MICROCOMPUTING AND QUALITATIVE DATA ANALYSIS

This book is dedicated to the memory of Renata Tesch

Microcomputing and Qualitative Data Analysis

ANNA WEAVER AND PAUL ATKINSON
School of Social and Administrative Studies
University of Wales
Cardiff

Avebury

Aldershot · Brookfield USA · Hong Kong · Singapore · Sydney

CDL001

© A. Weaver and P. Atkinson   1994

Published by
Avebury
Ashgate Publishing Company
Gower House
Croft Road
Aldershot
Hants GU11 3HR

Ashgate Publishing Company
Old Post Road
Brookfield
Vermont 05036
USA

307

W113

British Library Cataloguing in Publication Data

Weaver, Anna
  Microcomputing and Qualitative Data
  Analysis. - (Cardiff Papers in
  Qualitative Research)
  I. Title   II. Atkinson, Paul   III. Series
  300.72
  ISBN 1 85628 576 6

Library of Congress Cataloging-in-Publication Data

Weaver, Anna
    Microcomputing and qualitative data analysis / Anna Weaver and
Paul Atkinson.
      p. cm. -- (Cardiff papers in qualitative research)
    Includes bibliographical references   (p.   )
    ISBN 1-85628-576-6 : £32.00 ($58.95 U.S. : est.)
    1. Sociology--Research--Data processing. 2. IBM-compatible
computers. I. Atkinson, Paul. II. Title. III. Series.
HM24.W38 1994
300'.72--dc20   94-26910
                                                 CIP

Printed in Great Britain by Ipswich Book Co. Ltd., Ipswich,
Suffolk

Contents

Figures

Acknowledgements

The research on which this book is based was supported by an award from the Economic and Social Research Council, no. R-000-23-3200. We gratefully acknowledge the Council's support. The views expressed here are our own and not those of the Research Council. We would like to thank our colleagues at Cardiff, especially Martin Read for his help and advice, and Sara Delamont and Pete Davies for their comments on earlier drafts. Finally, we are grateful to Julius Roth for sharing his data with the community of ethnographers.

Introduction

Qualitative research in the social sciences is not unitary. Spread across different disciplines, it is concerned with different research strategies, and different kinds of data. This short monograph is not intended to address all aspects of qualitative data analysis, the variety of which has been captured by Silverman (1993) among others. It is not intended to be a prescriptive textbook of research methods and principles. We have tried to avoid recapitulating other books in the same general area (e.g., Tesch, 1990; Dey, 1993). Rather, we attempt to review a number of strategies for the analysis of qualitative data using microcomputers. This is an area of qualitative research that has expanded in recent years, and there is urgent need for the critical appraisal of the various opportunities that have been opened up.

This book, therefore, is intended to be a contribution to such a methodological task. The research on which it is based was unusual in conception, and restricted in focus. It was apparent to us that there has been huge growth recently of interest in so-called Computer Aided Qualitative Data Analysis ('CAQDAS'). Over the past decade computer software has been used to an increased extent for qualitative analysis. Several applications have been developed specifically for the purpose of qualitative data analysis, while generic software of various kinds has been used for various complementary analytic tasks.

The field is marked by diversity, and there is room for considerable confusion. There is need for clarification and systematic appraisal of options. At present there is considerable overlap and duplication between major software packages. While no researcher or research group will ever need to acquire and master all the available software, it is necessary for principled choices to be made as between alternative strategies. Fielding (1993) is among the recent commentators to call for systematic review and evaluation. Fielding suggests that the uncritical adoption and implementation of microcomputer software - or indeed the wholesale endorsement of the general approach - may commit the researcher to an implicit and uncritical adoption of particular analytic strategies.

1

Hitherto a number of authors have written about the general benefits of Computer Assisted Qualitative Data Analysis, and most of them have written about particular software. (Often those authors have been associated directly with the development and distribution of the software itself.) We shall make reference to some of those contributions throughout the book. Hitherto, however, there have been few attempts to undertake systematic comparison of analytic strategies supported by specific software, or of the fundamental methodological issues involved. There is a continuing need for critical reflection by analysts of their own implementation of microcomputing strategies. The methodological literature - to which this is intended to be a contribution - needs to go well beyond advice on particular programs and their implementation. Likewise, it needs more than endorsements of specific software packages from those who developed them or those who have used them successfully for their own analytic needs.

Here, therefore, we report on just one attempt to undertake a systematic comparison of complementary and contrasting strategies for the computer-assisted analysis of qualitative data. Before the more detailed presentation of our rationale and approach in the chapters that follow, we here provide a brief characterization of the project. Unlike the great majority of published contributions to this field, our own is grounded neither in one software package nor in an original piece of data collection and analysis. The project on which this is based was designed primarily in methodological terms, and was aimed entirely at critical reflection on the methodological implications of various current approaches. The core of our work, therefore, consists of a systematic review of microcomputing strategies, rather than a comprehensive review of all the available software and how to use it.

In formulating our approach to the evaluation of computing strategies, we decided to avoid working on data of our own. We acknowledge that the secondary analysis of qualitative data has its own very real drawbacks and limitations. Nevertheless, we believed that it would be of considerable benefit to be able to distance ourselves from the data and the outcome of the analysis. Approaching the data 'cold' was likely to free us to look dispassionately at the processes of data searching and analysis rather than at specific outputs.

Consequently, rather than basing our work on ethnographic fieldwork and data of our own, we decided to undertake a secondary analysis of an existing set of qualitative data. This research strategy held out two obvious advantages: we could use data we ourselves had not analyzed systematically before, and we could subject the same data to the various microcomputing strategies that we identified for exploration. While such secondary analysis can rarely approximate the full ethnographic experience of working with one's own data, grounded in memory and personal experience of the field, we believe that in this instance the strategy paid off. It helped us to compare the outputs of our own analytic strategies using different kinds of software, and to compare the outcomes with the published results based on those same data.

The data used for this research exercise were fieldnotes collected by Julius Roth in the course of his research on social relations in tuberculosis sanitaria. Roth's work is especially well known as a classic example of a sociologist turning personal adversity to professional advantage, in that having contracted TB he kept a journal of his experiences as an in-patient. He also undertook a period of fieldwork as a full participant, employed as an attendant in a hospital. He also undertook ethnographic fieldwork an overt researcher. His research is a particularly valuable case-study, in that he published a monograph (Roth, 1963) and a series of research papers (e.g. Roth, 1957). In addition, and most importantly for this project, Roth also made copies of his field data available to some fellow scholars for methodological purposes. As the data for our computer-assisted analyses we used the notes derived from Roth's period of work as a hospital attendant. The data had already been edited in the interests of confidentiality: Roth had already substituted pseudonyms, for example. The edited fieldnotes were derived from one hundred days of participant observation. They had been mimeographed and bound into a volume of several hundred pages. We did not attempt to reproduce the entire corpus of data. Rather, we sampled on the basis of days of the original fieldwork. The notes we selected were word-processed into text files - one file per day of fieldwork - and were then transformed into ASCII files, ready for importation into any of our chosen software.

It was, therefore, a particular feature of our own research that we came to the data 'cold'. Roth had made the data available to Atkinson some years before, and they had been used for teaching purposes in the interim. Weaver, on the other hand, began the project unfamiliar with the data. She was also unfamiliar with Roth's published work; Atkinson had read the publications beforehand. But neither tried to study Roth's publications closely before embarking on the project. We were not, after all, attempting to replicate or to test Roth's original research and his interpretations. Rather, we wished to capitalize on his previous generosity and use Roth's data almost exclusively for our own methodological purposes. For that reason, we were not preoccupied with trying to produce the 'best' analysis of the data, nor even to attempt a comprehensive analysis. Our use of a 'cold' set of data also freed us from the need to justify the data themselves - as we might have had they been our own - by producing particular kinds of analysis. The use of secondary analysis thus allowed us to concentrate on the microcomputing strategies themselves, and so to subordinate the substantive issues.

As we have indicated, the problems of secondary analysis of ethnographic data are well recognized. Our distance from the data was undoubtedly liberating. It was, however, a source of limitations. When one reads fieldnotes or transcripts, tacit knowledge is inevitably brought to bear. In most ethnographic projects the analyst draws on his or her personal experience of 'the field'. Reading and re-reading the fieldnotes is an active, interpretative process. One reads knowledge and experience into the notes and the other data. In the course of this project, on the other hand, we were relying on 'the data' alone, which as a consequence often felt 'empty' or 'thin'. Because we were working in this way, we were not able to evaluate and exemplify the procedures whereby data may be coded and analyzed concurrently with fieldwork. Since we were not collecting the data, we were obviously not able to develop a fully 'grounded' approach whereby our emerging categories and theories could inform further data collection. In the course of real research projects, the close linkage between data analysis and fieldwork is important; here we cannot address that issue explicitly.

In setting about our work we wanted to documentand to reflect on various complementary and contrasting strategies for CAQDAS. We identified a number of basic approaches to computer-based analysis, and focused on particular software packages that would exemplify them. We therefore have made no attempt to give equal attention to all the available software. For more 'consumer-oriented' reviews and comparisons the reader must look elsewhere (e.g. Tesch, 1990). In designing our project we also imposed a further limitation. We chose to operate entirely in an MS-DOS/Windows environment, working exclusively on IBM-compatible PCs. We therefore excluded software designed exclusively for mainframe computers, and also those for Macintosh machines. To some extent that decision was an arbitrary one, reflecting the computing environment we happened to be working in at Cardiff. To some extent it also reflected the fact that, in the UK at any rate, PCs are the most widely used machines. Whatever the intrinsic merits of the machines and their associated software, there is little doubt that there is currently the greatest mileage in a coherent array of software, all designed for compatibility with one operating system.

We shall begin by contrasting two complementary strategies, each exemplified by one application. We begin with the software that is almost certainly the most widely implemented at the present time - ETHNOGRAPH. That is based on a strategy of 'coding' and allows the analyst to segment the text (fieldnotes, interview transcripts and the like) into chunks, and mark them with codes representing their analytical significance. By coding and segmenting the data in this way, we are able to manipulate text in various ways. The program can search for data marked with the same code and, since a number of codes can be attached to the same segment, it can also search for chunks of text marked with two or more specified codes. Coded chunks retrieved in such searches can then be relocated in analytic files for further scrutiny. It is, therefore, properly referred to as a 'code-and-retrieve' approach. The ETHNOGRAPH software (Seidel, 1988) is an important starting-point. It is, we suspect, the 'application of choice' for many contemporary researchers and research groups. In many contexts 'analysis' seems to be treated as synonymous with 'coding' the data, and the ETHNOGRAPH satisfies the need of researchers who wish to implement such an approach.

The code-and-retrieve approach contrasts with those that focus on the 'indigenous' terms in fieldnotes, transcribed interactions and interviews. Rather than adding code words to segments of text, the analyst searches on the lexicon of the text files themselves. There are many generic programmes

4

that can be used for such purposes. They include a number of applications intended for 'keyword-in-context' and content-analysis. There is no need for applications bespoke for qualitative sociological or anthropological data. We have illustrated the approach using FYI3000PLUS, a particularly powerful and flexible exemplar of this class of software. The lexical searching strategy is especially useful for analyzing interview transcripts, or in types of research where researchers want to examine the informants' own use of language. Alternatively, it may supplement other techniques, aiding the process whereby analytical categories are constructed, or for checking the comprehensive coverage of topics. In the latter respect, lexical searching and coding are clearly complementary strategies for interrogating the data.

We also give consideration to software that attempts to go beyond code-and-retrieve and lexical searching. They are intended to facilitate 'theory-building' and the representation of 'grounded theory'. Here we exemplify such approaches with KWALITAN, software originally developed in the Netherlands, and NUDIST, which originated in Australia and is now widely disseminated. In somewhat different ways these applications attempt to introduce a 'value-added' element to the use of the microcomputer. On the other hand, they - like the ETHNOGRAPH and other software like it - remain rooted in the manual techniques of data storage and retrieval that pre-date the introduction of computer software. In suggesting this we do not wish to belittle the software or to deny their value. The coding approaches are supported in a more comprehensive and efficient way than is possible manually; the search functions go beyond what is possible manually. One could not hope to search large bodies of text manually in the way that bulk indexing or keyword-in-context programs do. The so-called theory-building programs allow us to do things that could not be done with the physical marking and filing of textual data. Our point is, rather, about the conceptual basis for such operations.

We finally consider some applications and a strategy that seem to offer some genuinely novel uses of computing. This strategy uses the capacities of Hypertext software, which we exemplify with GUIDE, a commercially available program. This software - again, not specifically designed for use with qualitative social research - allows the analyst to create complex pathways and linkages within the data, and between the ethnographic text files and other data or other media. Hypertext software, such as GUIDE, is intended to support a new approach to both reading and writing texts. Hence hypertext has implications for the humanities, and several important texts have examined its implications for subjects such as literary and cultural theory (Bolter, 1991; Landow, 1992). Since the analysis of qualitative data consists of complex interactive processes of reading and writing, it seems possible that hypertext will also offer new opportunities for the conduct of analysis.

The general hypertext model implies analytic strategies that are specific to a computing environment. It also creates the possibility of thinking about writing ethnography as well as analyzing data. Indeed, the hypertext strategy breaks down distinctions between 'data', 'analysis' and 'presentation'. Ultimately, the possibilities of hypertext and hypermedia may allow the 'reader' of ethnography to interact with information of diverse sorts, in highly flexible ways, and with an active involvement in the exploration of data or commentary. The sequence of research tasks we undertook meant that when we came to work with the hypertext application we had already developed many ideas and hypotheses about the data. That undoubtedly coloured our own experience of hypertext as a strategy. Nevertheless, we believe that there are real possibilities and advantages to be explored in this particular area. Indeed, we suggest that the hypertext strategy may conceivably transform the way ethnographers think about the research process and its outcomes. We do not wish to overstate the case here: hypertext in and of itself does not revolutionize the processes of reading and writing. We do believe, however, that ethnographers who wish to explore the possibilities of contemporary computing should pay serious attention to the possibilities of hypertext applications. Although we do not go into further discussion of the possibilities in this book, the hypertext strategy may be taken a stage further, to incorporate a 'hypermedia' approach. As Thomas (1993, p. 1) suggests,

> Using hypertext, a researcher could include not only a conventional description of the method of a study, but also graphics (photos or video segments) and sound to illustrate or clarify procedures. Qualitative researchers may find hypertext especially helpful, since they would be able to include, on a palm-sized disk, the anecdotes illustrating concepts, as well as the actual interview segments from which data were drawn.

Thomas also goes on to say

> Imagine the richness of data if Becker's study of marijuana users, Manning's accounts of narcotics agents, or Irwin's analysis of prison culture included 3-D visuals and sound. This kind of communication would not only infuse ethnographic texts with richer detail, it would add a new level of accountability by giving the reader a view of the context from which the data and analysis derived.

A hypertext strategy remains expensive to implement, and it is not an easy option. For many researchers and research groups, it is probably not a feasible option currently. It is, however, an approach that deserves serious consideration on methodological grounds. It may, we suspect, assume increasing importance in the social sciences in the near future.

In general, we do not endorse a technological fix for the future of ethnography. The conceptual and methodological issues are far too serious and complex for that. We do believe, however, that qualitative research in the social sciences must continue to be informed by a general and well-informed awareness of the possibilities of modern computing. Equally, there is need for care and caution. Any enthusiasm for microcomputing applications must be tempered with a full appreciation of their broader methodological implications. The reasons for such a balanced and critical approach to CAQDAS, and some of the issues which researchers need to pay attention to, will be the focus of the next chapter, as well as informing the entire book.

1 Microcomputing and qualitative analysis

Introduction

As many writers have observed (e.g., Richards and Richards, 1991a, p. 38; 1991b, p. 238; Walker and Bryman, 1991, pp. 3-4; Walker, 1993, p. 92), there is little cumulative methodological discourse on qualitative data handling processes, and this has meant computers being introduced into the field with very little systematic attention to their significance. (Ironically, it is believed that the codification of qualitative method is one potential advantage of the introduction of computers (Conrad and Reinharz 1984, p. 6).) This problem is perpetuated by the tendency where, although authors recognize the lack of critical discussion on 'what impact the mechanical assistance offered by any computer program may have on the methods of thought' (Walker, 1993, p. 92), little has been done to fill this gap in methodological literature. Instead, discourse on microcomputing and qualitative methods reflects other concerns. This chapter will first focus on these general concerns, and then attempt to reconstruct some of the more detailed issues that have hitherto been raised.

According to Pfaffenberger (1988, pp. 14-5), two conflicting approaches dominate the bulk of discourse on microcomputing and qualitative analysis. The first approach, which he terms 'technological somnambulism', is essentially utilitarian, with computers being viewed simply as material tools. If this position is adopted, serious methodological reflection is rendered unnecessary: writers have focused on the technical capabilities of particular programs, emphasizing their efficiency. A contrasting approach, however, does not view the computer as an acultural, apolitical, amoral tool. From this perspective of 'technnological determinism', writers have attributed technology with a causal power on social and cultural life, and fear that computers may erode some of the most celebrated aspects of qualitative research since they 'pose the threat of dehumanization, mechanization, quantification, and the sterilization of all that is warm and cuddly in human nature' (Pfaffenberger, 1988, p. 10).

9

However, for Pfaffenberger, both attitudes misunderstand the impact of computers because they do not recognize the inherently social character of technology:

> Every technology is constructed in a social setting and a cultural environment. Woven into its material fabric are tacit social and cultural assumptions, such as a typification of the user, the social setting in which the technology will be used, the knowledge that the user will bring to the machine, and more. (Pfaffenberger, 1988, p. 10)

Pfaffenberger argues that these ideas are embodied in genres of software and that, whereas individual programs come and go, these are transcendental. Thus, it is upon the genres of software that methodological discourse must focus. However, perhaps it is only through the detailed study of particular programs, representing the various genres, that knowledge about their underlying assumptions can emerge. That is the position adopted in this book.

Publications of recent years have taken on board the social nature of technology, and do not express either the extreme elements of 'technophobia' or 'somnambulism' identified by Pfaffenberger. But there is a tendency to focus on either technical issues, on the one hand, or methodological ones, on the other.

The technical approach

Many writers have focused on the technical capabilities of programs. This is not necessarily because they do not recognize the possible impact of computer tools upon analytical thought, but rather that they see the former as having the potential to free the latter. For example, the fact that the computer 'doesn't get tired and miss sections of data when it analyzes' (Agar, 1983, p. 26), is a clear technical advantage of the computer over the human mind, and one which is bound to have methodological consequences. Freeing the researcher of the most mechanical and mundane organizational and analytical tasks, conserves energy for interpretative work. Furthermore, computer tools encourage self assessment: 'the only effect of using software for analysis, with respect to orderliness, is to make the already-methodological researcher more clearly aware of the procedures used, since the process becomes more explicit' (Tesch, 1989, p. 150). Renata Tesch (1989; 1990; 1991) is one of the leading authors in this field. Her book (Tesch 1990) is probably the most useful and comprehensive text for qualitative researchers who are interested in how their analytic needs may be met by available technology. Tesch's book basically consists of two parts: the first describes a wide selection of analytical traditions in qualitative sociological, psychological and educational research; the second describes the software which may accommodate these various interests.

Tesch's book makes both explicit and implicit statements about a particular methodological position regarding the relation between qualitative analysis and software tools - one which is shared by many enthusiasts in this area. She explicitly argues that her book is designed to be an information source - a means of making decisions about methods and tools on the basis of technical characteristics (1990, p. 5). Thus the focus is on technical rather than epistemological issues. More implicitly, the order in which these sections appear has an underlying message: the researcher begins with a style of analysis and then fits a program to fit its needs - not vice versa.

However, despite Tesch's obvious position in this debate as an enthusiast for CAQDAS, the way in which she approaches the subject matter, in both content and style, may be interpreted in a more negative light. Her treatise may be interpreted as a rigorous, obsessive piece of work which over-systematizes qualitative methods, and pigeonholes techniques in a way which does not reflect their 'messy' reality in practice. Furthermore, nowhere does Tesch provide a critique of qualitative methods, or give attention to their more theoretical or reflective aspects. The focus is exclusively technical: the technical demands of analysis imposed by various approaches and the technical solutions offered by various software. The attitude reflected in Tesch's work is precisely what many researchers believe to be a negative effect of microcomputing on qualitative analysis. Thus, ironically, the fact that a book promoting CAQDAS exhibits those (undesirable) characteristics, may be taken as evidence of the 'technical culture', as described by Lyman (1984), taking its toll on the way researchers think - not only about their data, but also about their method.

Indeed, it seems that Tesch's work, like that of many enthusiasts in this area, exhibits an attitude which is produced by, and helps to reproduce, this technical culture. In this culture, the computer seen essentially as a material tool which is completely dominated by a human user. This attitude is articulated and reinforced by the language surrounding computers. For example:

> The computer is frequently given a female gender in everyday speech ("she's crashed three times today"). By appropriating the language of gender domination to the "man/machine" relation, technical culture is able to give the computer an image of being cooperatively subordinate and non-threatening because easily controlled by masculinity. This is why the language of control is filled with male military/game slang and jargon ... (Lyman, 1984, p. 81)

However, such jargon is, according to Lyman, essentially ideological because it is through the language surrounding computers that the technical culture is reproduced.

In any case, Tesch's work certainly needs to be complemented by an evaluation of software which is more sensitive to methodological as opposed to technical issues. To tackle this in the present book, the structure of her work has been turned upon its head, as it were. It begins with a computing strategy, or rather a specific program within a generic strategy, and then examine the kinds of analytic strategies it encourages and discourages, and the kind of relationship that develops between researcher and data.

Some of these issues have been considered to a more satisfactory degree by authors of a more recent volume, edited by Fielding and Lee (1991). This collection of papers focuses on several themes, ranging from technical information about software (the area of Tesch's expertise), the role of computers in teaching, to the implications of computing for the 'craft' of qualitative research.

The methodological approach

Richards and Richards (1991a, p. 39) argue that the significance of microcomputers for qualitative analysis is not restricted to improved efficiency: they have had an impact which is much more profound. Indeed, they assert that this new technology has brought about a 'methodological revolution'. They argue that this has three aspects. First, it reshapes the research process, fundamentally altering the experience of research. Second, it challenges the conventional dichotomy of qualitative and quantitative research methods. Finally, it challenges the differences between various types of qualitative method. One problem potential problem here is:

> Not only do computer techniques gloss over differences in method: they also may flatten them out. Researchers will design their projects to fit known programs, and most programs are good at a limited set of tasks. (Richards and Richards, 1991a, pp. 42-3).

This, they argue elsewhere, will result in a 'new form of what Wax (1971) described as the "cage" of commitment to particular data gathering methods' (1991b, p. 238). Thus, the Richards see the fit between analysis techniques and programs as more problematic than does Tesch. Such methodological issues will now be examined in more detail, with particular reference to three distinct analytical strategies (manifest in three types of generic software) which direct the focus of this book: coding segments, lexical searching, and hypertext.

The dichotomy between qualitative and qualitative research

One aspect of the methodological revolution, brought about by the introduction of computers into qualitative research, is a challenge to the conventional dichotomy between quantitative and qualitative research methods (Richards and Richards, 1991a, p. 39). However, this is a difficult argument to assess one way or the other since there is no unified 'qualitative method' as such; researchers apply different meanings to the term, and thus there are differences in the way the conventional relation between qualitative and quantitative research has been interpreted. This difficulty is further complicated by the problem, noted earlier, that there is a general lack of discourse on qualitative analysis. There remains in some quarters the belief that techniques such as 'verstehen' and ethnography cannot really be taught, but only learned through experience. Procedures in quantitative research, however, have been much more widely documented. Nevertheless, this section attempts to outline some of the issues regarding the challenges posed by microcomputers to some of the more conventional aspects of qualitative and quantitative methods

Rigour and standardization

Some writers have argued that one change in the relation between qualitative and quantitative analysis incurred by microcomputers is the possibility of greater rigour in the former. This change has been interpreted in various ways. One approach is that, in principle, qualitative and quantitative research have always had similarities regarding their analytical goals. For example, Becker, Gordon and LeBailly (1984, pp. 20-1), argue that both traditions have the same goals of constructing and testing propositions, of assuring that some systematic routine has been followed and that all evidence has been considered in this process. The difference, they maintain, lies in the means that these ends are achieved. In this context, the introduction of software for qualitative analysis has been optimistically received since it allows the researcher to be more thorough in the search and retrieval of negating, as well as supporting, evidence. Computers have also challenged another difference between qualitative and quantitative approaches to research: the standardization of method. Since analytical methods are not standardized in qualitative research, and microcomputing provides new ways of standardizing methods, this technology is considered desirable.

Thus, for Becker et al. (1984), the chief impact of microcomputing upon the relation between the two research traditions is to make it more symmetrical in terms of rigour and standardization. However, many researchers have displayed reservations about the latter, arguing that methodological diversity should be celebrated (for example Richards and Richards, 1991a, p. 43). This mixture of responses seems to be due partly to the ambiguous relation between the 'standardization' and 'codification' of qualitative methods, which needs to be seen in context of the history of qualitative methodology.

One important achievement of its evolution (which has coincided with 'postmodern' critiques of universal reason) was to challenge the assumption that there is one truth, or one acceptable form or method of knowing, or standard/universal criteria against which knowledge can be measured. In this context, the threat of microcomputers encouraging standardization would be an unwelcome development.

A second important value of qualitative methodology is reflexivity or self-awareness (as will be discussed later in this chapter). However, this has been at odds with the tendency of much research to remain vague about methods of analysis when imparting findings to others. In addition to diminishing reflexivity, the lack of codification of method in qualitative research (or the tendency for analytic methods to remain private, mysterious, idiosyncratic, and simplistic) poses problems for the communication of research and the teaching of social research methods. Microcomputers may help to resolve this situation however: with the advent of computers in the field, 'we should be able to codify exactly how we analyze our data and to reproduce our analytic steps' in ways that serve these interests (Conrad and Reinharz, 1984, p. 6).

There are several levels or stages of analysis which may be codified. First, as noted by Conrad and Reinharz, CAQDAS in itself signifies 'a rudimentary codification of analytic procedures'. Second, the printing of each analytic phase (or its preservation as a file on disk), such as a search for a code, helps codification to continue throughout analysis. A similar point is made by Read (1990, p. 507) in relation of computer art. He argues that, not only can an artist's end product be preserved as a thing in itself, but also the steps taken by the artist may be preserved and reproduced, as a way of showing development of conceptualization. The same may be possible with the construction of an ethnography.

However, there is a fear that the codification of analytical procedures facilitated by computers (at both levels identified by Conrad and Reinharz), will bring about a standardization of procedures, and that this will involve a closing of the diversity of approaches. First, it is feared that programs themselves represent codification which standardizes analytic techniques: 'Some feel that the assumptions built into available programs represent a hidden form of closure around a particular view of qualitative analysis' (Fielding and Lee, 1991, p. 73). Furthermore, if the assumptions underlying software represent only a handful of analytical strategies, these methods will be codified or even standardized at the expense of others, resulting in the extinction of potentially valuable techniques. If this has already happened, it would be the coding segments strategy which has enjoyed this dominant position in software utilized for qualitative sociological research.

Similarly, it must not be assumed that researchers will want to divulge their methods of analysis or stages of thought as described by Read (1990), especially if they feel that they have taken an unconventional or unusual approach. Such measures increase the research's vulnerability, since the critic will be empowered and able to penetrate in new ways, not only the final product, but also the stages that shaped its final form. This is perhaps particularly salient with hypertext where codification is much more accessible to the reader, and where consequences for the power relation between reader and writer are much more profound. Reactions to this possibility may go either way, but it certainly seems that there is potentially a 'dark side' of codification and that minority methods may be discouraged as a result.

Rather than simply rendering qualitative method more thorough, codified, and standardized, it has been argued that the introduction of computers into the field has challenged the relation between qualitative and quantitative research in more fundamental ways. Put simply, it has provoked changes in qualitative method which narrow the conventional gap between the two approaches of analysis. For example, Ragin and Becker (1989) argue that technological advances in tools for qualitative analysis are, in effect, closing the gap between 'variable' and 'case-oriented' research. Whereas quantitative research has typically been interested in explaining variability across cases, qualitative research has become renowned for comprehending variability within a single case (Ragin and Becker, 1989, p. 50). Seidel, the creator of ETHNOGRAPH, takes a similar view. In an essay considering the 'dark side' of applying computers to qualitative research, he notes that new forms of 'analytic madness' may be introduced into the field as a result (Seidel, 1991, p. 107). In particular, those changes in technique associated with increased volume and diversity, which are encouraged by the use of microcomputers, directly challenge the gap between qualitative and quantitative methods.

Volume and diversity

Seidel has noted a tendency in research for a fascination with volume, and that the computer feeds this tendency, making it more feasible - especially in qualitative research. Seidel recognizes that this, in itself, is not necessarily a bad thing. What is important, however, is that researchers do not overstep what is practical and allow a new type of 'fetishism' with volume take hold (Seidel, 1991, p. 109). This fetishism is also reflected in other behaviours whereby the significance of a phenomenon is judged by the number of times it occurs in the data. Thus it is equally important that such activities do not become conflated with 'analysis' since, as noted by Seidel (1991, p. 113), '[m]any times a single occurrence of something is more important, theoretically and analytically, than multiple occurrences of something'.

There is a related 'madness' of fascination with distribution: to discover and account for variations across a large number of sites. Thus, not only does the introduction of computers enable the analysis of a large volume of data for a single case, but also a large volume of data for a number of cases. Seidel warns that this concern with distribution may be displacing the distinctive concern of qualitative research to reveal the structure and intricacies of particular sites, since the 'superficial glosses' of a large number of cases diminishes the time dedicated to analyzing specific ones (Seidel, 1991, p. 110). In his own words:

> My concern is that, because computer technology allows us to deal with large volumes of data, we will be lured into analytic practices and conceptual problems more conducive to breadth analysis rather than depth analysis. We will start trading off resolution for scope. (Seidel, 1991, p. 112)

Thus, in sum, Seidel argues that the introduction of computer assisted analysis in qualitative research makes it easier for researchers to integrate methods previously limited to the domain of quantitative research. But the issue is for what reasons these methods are used, and whether the researcher is aware of the decision to use these methods. The danger seems to lie in the possibility of this decision being implicit to the extent that it is not recognized as one at all. If the researcher begins to assume that this is the 'natural', 'commensense', or even 'only' way to analyze qualitative material, conventions of qualitative method will be threatened.

The authority of science and technology

It is possible that the tendencies identified by Ragin and Becker (1989) and Seidel (1991) stem from a particular set of epistemological assumptions about what constitutes knowledge. Moreover, perhaps these assumptions, which seem to have infiltrated qualitative research since the introduction of computer technology, are bound up with a particular set of ideas about what constitutes 'scientific' knowledge - one conventionally associated with quantitative research. Quantitative knowledge has for a long time enjoyed a privileged position in many disciplines, and despite the increasing popularity of qualitative approaches since the 1960s, it still retains a dominant position both in the academic community and in discourses of everyday life. In other words, concerns with volume and distribution may reflect a wider concern of adding scientific validity to qualitative studies. At an even wider level, the motive for introducing computers into qualitative research may be bound up with attempts to 'clean up' the tradition, making it more systematic, standardized, and generally rendering its knowledge claims more acceptable to the scientific community and the 'gatekeepers' of research:

> Undoubtedly, some of the enthusiasm seen in the United States for computer-assisted field research arises out of a concern to destigmatize qualitative research in an environment which is not entirely sympathetic towards it, by finding ways to make qualitative research look more scientific. (Fielding and Lee, 1991, pp. 6-7)

At a more micro level, there is another way in which the authority of science, and the prestige of technology, may affect qualitative analysis. This is to do with the style in which computers do things, and the nature of the things they produce. The printed page, for example, gives an instant authority to computer input and output. Comparing the respective natures of keyboarding and handwriting, Altheide (1985, pp. 97-9) argues that 'handwriting, which involves flow and rhythm, reveals more about its temporal production'. By contrast, there is no reflection of mood in printed writing, and this makes 'keyboard products appear to be essentially context free, and therefore more objective'. Furthermore, Altheide argues that keyboarding is a social form which both reflects and directs formal, technical rationality.

This may have many effects. Firstly, the objective, context free status of fieldnotes may cause them to become depersonalized and alienated from the researcher. Secondly, when printed font dominates the thinking inherent to reading and writing in the whole process of analysis, rather than merely in the phase of writing up results, perhaps we are less likely to question our ideas and conclusions that drive the analysis. A similar phenomenon, noted by Richards and Richards (1991a, p. 49), is that the 'neat retrieval process' conducted by the computer, distances researchers from the 'messy original data'. This may lead the researcher into a 'false sense of security' regarding the characterization of the data. For this reason, retaining links to the original data (including handwritten notes) throughout the analysis is of vital importance.

The extent of these phenomena will, of course, differ with the specific characteristics of programs. For example, with ETHNOGRAPH, the researcher is encouraged to write marginal comments and code manually on the hard copy of data independently of the computer whereas, with KWALITAN, NUDIST and GUIDE, all analyses are entered directly into the computer. However, the latter group make the second condition, of retaining links with original (uncoded) data, more accessible to the researcher than does ETHNOGRAPH.

Holism, context, and cultures of knowledge

Blank (1988, p. 3) draws a parallel between the roles of the literary critic and the ethnographer, regarding the relation of each to their respective narratives:

> The primary characteristic of narrative text is that it is structured by the author. To understand narrative as the author intended involves a holistic understanding of the entire text as the context within which individual portions of the text require meaning and significance. Similarly, case-oriented research strategies try to grasp social processes and events as wholes.

Like the literary narrative is constructed by the author, narratives of everyday life are intersubjectively authored by social actors, interactions and events. Likewise, field events only make sense in the context of particular narratives (Gergen and Gergen, 1991), and thus many social researchers argue that qualitative research is essentially about understanding data in their fieldnote context (or phenomena in their social context), as an interconnected whole (or interacting life-worlds that constitute everyday life in a particular field). However, since many computer assisted analyses involve the generation of a large body of recontextualized data, it becomes increasingly difficult for the researcher to recall their original context in fieldnotes.

This is due to an apparent paradox between the holistic aims of much research, on the one hand, and the 'coding' strategy, most commonly utilized

17

by computer programs for qualitative analysis, on the other. This particular principle of organization, with its contingent loss of contextual information, seems to conflict with the goal of holism. This contradiction is noted by Wagner (1989, p. 420) who writes: 'computerization of qualitative data, and the pigeon-holing it normally implies, runs counter to a disciplinary perspective that sees the whole as greater than the sum of its parts'. Both Wagner and Read seem to stress the importance of the other side of Gadamer's 'hermeneutic circle': the part must be understood in terms of the whole, as well as the whole in terms of the part.

Although this parallel arguably holds between the literary critic and the ethnographer (or case-oriented researcher), it does not hold between the former and the variable-oriented researcher. For this type of research involves a very different kind of approach to data and interpretation, irrespective of whether they are text or numbers. By imposing a conceptual order onto data, researchers classify them into general categories (i.e. variables). Events are thereby extracted from their original idiosyncratic contexts in fieldnotes.

The variable-oriented approach is part of a 'technical culture', and it is this technical culture which seems to be reflected in most of the software designed for qualitative analysis. Here, the original structure of data is secondary to the problem of conceptual structure, in terms of which data are to be recontextualized. More specifically, programs that adopt the coding segments strategy, are more complementary to variable-oriented research than the 'narrative culture' characterizing traditional ethnography. The extent to which this argument is applicable obviously varies with different genres of software for qualitative analysis.

The hypertext strategy, for example, promises a mode of organization that remains more faithful to the narrative culture than do chunking and coding techniques. This has been shown by Walker (1993) who compared ETHNOGRAPH, representing the coding segments strategy, and MARTIN, representing hypertext. Analysis using ETHNOGRAPH consisted of 'labelling, searching for patterns, and eventual synthesis into categories ... much in the manner described by Miles and Huberman'. Use of MARTIN, however, 'facilitated not only a search for patterns but also yielded a product similar to the "thick description"' necessary for the understanding and interpretation of the meaning of experience (Walker, 1993, p. 109).

Walker (1993, p. 110) argues that the 'extra' provided by MARTIN lies in its richer contextual description, whereas the power of ETHNOGRAPH lies in its search and display facilities, as these provide greater support for the discovery of pattern in data. This seems to be a generic quality hypertext rather than one of this particular program, for Read (1990, p. 508) also argues that hypertext facilitates thick description:

> That software has the power to structure and restructure data, to be able to manipulate it at levels ranging from numeric to symbolic, and to organize and reorganize it in multiple ways and through multiple media

suggests the potential for being able to confront data at the level of its richness and multiplexity, not in a scaled-down, simplified, coded, thinned-out substitute.

Furthermore, Read continues, the sights and sounds of events may be incorporated into the ethnography itself so that they too become part of the thick description (p. 509), rather than their roles being limited only to its construction.

Thus, it may be deduced that Lyman's (1989) warning that hypertext systems belong to a technical culture, and that they enhance variable-oriented analytical strategies, is not the only possible interpretation. It seems equally possible that, because it enhances contextual description, hypertext can be used in a way that is more faithful to the 'narrative culture' of traditional ethnography than can previous genres of software.

Relation to text

An important concern about the introduction of computers is regarding its potential effect on the relation between researcher and data. It has been argued that there has been a tendency for software used in qualitative analysis to drive the researcher into the text, with an obsessive concern of organizing, searching, and retrieving the text in various ways (Richards and Richards, 1991a, p. 52). But, as noted by the same authors, how do such approaches to data analysis fit with the traditional demands of 'grounded theory', which is the goal of much contemporary sociological research? Richards and Richards argue that it is not a very comfortable one:

> Earlier computer programs tended to drive qualitative analysis much more into the text - either to words and their frequency of occurrence, or to segments indexed for retrieval. For linguistic analysis, this may be the required focus. But it can mean a surprizingly strong shift from what was the rhythm both of 'grounded theory' and of traditional ethnography - to get clear of the text. (Richards and Richards, 1991a, p. 52)

They believe that, in order to remain faithful to these traditions, analytical attention must rise above the text, so to speak, to explore coding or indexing systems - but without losing links to the text. In general, computer software has not encouraged this however. In this sense, the code and retrieval method adopted by much software detracts from the goals of grounded theory:

> To code and retrieve text is to cut it up. The 'grounded theory' method leaves text almost untouched. The researcher's contact with the data is light, hovering over the text and rethinking its meanings, then rising from it to comparative imaginative reflections. It is the difference

between the touch of scissors and that of a butterfly. (Richards and Richards, 1991b, p. 260)

Ironically, however, driving the analysis into the text does not necessarily facilitate a closer, tighter relationship between the researcher and data. For example, despite the honourable intentions of John Seidel for his program ETHNOGRAPH, researchers have reported that the program distances them from the data (Seidel 1991, p. 114). Thus, what needs to be established is whether it is ETHNOGRAPH in particular which causes this distancing, or whether it is a more generic problem attached to particular a computing strategy (coding segments), or even CAQDAS in general.

It may be argued that coding segments and lexical searching software are more in keeping with the techniques set out by Miles and Huberman (1984) than those set out by Glaser and Strauss (1967). Whereas it seems that hypertext software may encourage analytical strategies that are more faithful to the conventional relation between researcher and data in the grounded theory approach. Perhaps the following observation made by Lyman (1989, p. 79) may help to explain why:

> The relationship between the window of text and other sections may be seen only by "scrolling"; it is time-consuming to scroll other parts of the text, and, like a scroll, as one part is uncovered, another is covered. Thus the computer gives text a temporal structure, like a conversation, while printed pages are spatial and may be spread out to see the relationships between different parts of an argument.

This is an important point, and one which relates differently to various types of software. The coding segments strategy, as exemplified by ETHNOGRAPH, adopts a more spatial representation of data (data are analyzed on a hard copy), whereas hypertext encourages a more temporal approach to text (data are analyzed online so that the researcher's attention can only be focussed on one section of text at any one time). Lyman also notes that, because when using a computer for reading and writing attention is focused on the window, the drift in the humanities away from explanation and towards hermeneutic description will be reinforced.

Reification and reflexivity

It has been noted that the terms 'coding' and 'analysis' have become conflated (Atkinson, 1991). However, despite its prevalence in program manuals and methodological discourse, this term is problematic. In fact, one problem with the term is a form of 'analytical madness' for Seidel (1991, p. 112). This is 'the reification of the relationship between the researcher and data' which he sees as being exacerbated by computers. The problem here is with conceptual processes of assigning codes to identify segments of text. Indeed, Seidel now regrets using the terms 'codeword' and 'coding' to articulate the analysis process with ETHNOGRAPH. He says of the term 'codeword':

> The problem I have with it is the epistemological assumptions that researchers bring to it. For many researchers, identifying and naming things that they find in their data is assumed to be a simple, straightforward, unproblematic process. (Seidel, 1991, p. 112)

Seidel argues that researchers must be reflexive, and raise epistemological questions during the coding process. For example, does that identified as significant in the data (and therefore tagged with a code) really exist, or is it an artefact of a 'strange and peculiar relationship' between the researcher and his/her data? Moreover, there is little recognition of the contingencies that affect this relationship, such as the 'conceptual and intellectual baggage' carried by the researcher to the field, or practical problems which have to be resolved when dealing with the data (Seidel, 1991, p. 112). Richards and Richards (1991b, p. 246) make a similar point about reification: the 'assumption is often made that themes are there waiting to be freed and that we will, of course, recognize an emerging theme as such as we see it happen'.

Thus, perhaps the coding strategy implicitly encourages researchers to be less reflexive about their analyses. However, the issues of reification and reflexivity are not the same for other strategies of data analysis in qualitative research. Other strategies may encourage more reflexivity than chunking and coding software, or perhaps a combination of strategies may facilitate greater methodological conscientiousness.

For example, a combination of the coding segments and lexical strategies may offset the tendencies described by Seidel (1991). Richards and Richards (1991b, p. 243) argue that computers should facilitate access 'to what is in the text, not only to what the researcher says it is about' (as manifest in codes). They continue that, for most qualitative research, the 'noises' in data, or patterns in the words that construct a dialogue, are likely to be of analytic significance. Access to these 'noises' may help to keep in check the interpretations of the researcher.

However, perhaps the hypertext approach to data analysis promises the most revolutionary solution to these issues. The following statement perhaps applies more to hypertext than to any other strategy: 'The computer forces us now to recognize that texts themselves are variable, not "real", and that our apprehension of them can and should be probed in its own right' (White and Truex, 1988, p. 485). This is because the its representation of text is much more fluid. The researcher is able to restructure it in countless different ways, without having to remove it from its original context. Secondly, all decisions and connections are made explicit, as they are manifest in the actual structure of the database. Furthermore, it is possible, with hypertext software, to conceptually have two databases: one about the data, and one about the analysis, both of which are physically interconnected. Thus, if reflexivity is, as Escher proposed, 'a hand drawing the hand which is drawing' (Heisse, 1991, p. 136), hypertext encourages this reflective activity throughout the analysis.

Dynamic and static representations

If one takes the position of Seidel, that coded segments are artefacts of a relationship between researcher and data (rather than an intrinsic quality of the data themselves), there follows an apparent contradiction between the static nature of coded segments (the product), and the dynamic, fluid, processural nature of the relationship (the origin). For if the relationship between researcher and data is to be fluid and dynamic, considerable demands for flexibility are placed on codes and the way they organize data, in order to reflect and encourage this relationship. For as Christensen (1992, p. 5) notes of coding aiding conceptualization: 'The dynamic development of categories, as well as the ongoing overruling and replacement of codes and categories with new ones that are better fitting, is at the core of the method'. This problem has been taken seriously by programmers in the field, but with limited success. Thus, perhaps the representation and facilitation of knowledge in the form of coded segments will always be impaired to some extent. But, perhaps more importantly, what is needed is a methodological assessment of the coding segments strategy, so that researchers can make informed choice about whether such limitations may be of significance to their particular study.

It is especially important to explore whether other approaches to data analysis have as many limitations in this respect, or whether a combination of approaches can better accommodate the dynamic relation between the researcher and data. Richards and Richards (1991b, pp. 252-3) note the advantage of adopting a dual strategy of lexical searching and coding segments. As analysis and theory develop, new categories emerge. Ideally, this necessitates a recoding of data but, since this option is generally too expensive in terms of labour, these new categories will be applied only to those data not yet coded. 'Attention to this problem requires ways of locating the passages of already-indexed text where the new category is likely to have been useful' (Richards and Richards, 1991b, p. 252). They argue that a string search provides a useful method of doing this, facilitating a 'means to access belatedly identified themes in already-coded text'.

However, it must be emphasized that a lexical searching strategy offers more than simply reducing the pitfalls of coding. Obviously, it is invaluable to discourse and content analyses, but it is also a useful tool for invoking insights to process and change over space and time. For example, in literary studies, one use of a string search is to 'provide information for deciding whether a philosopher always means "x" by the searched for word or phrase, or never does, or sometimes does', or the development of an author's ideas (Burkholder, 1992, p. 6). Transferred to an ethnographic context, the same principle applies. For example, the ethnographer may want to examine if the amount of time spent in a TB hospital affects the way in which patients and staff conceptualize contamination. (Although this technique has limited use where dialogue is not directly or accurately recorded, as is often the case in fieldnote data.) Thus, a lexical searching strategy may be useful, not only for a synchronic snapshot of the use of words and phrases or the meanings attached to them, but also for a diachronic characterization of events.

However, as Richards and Richards (1991b, p. 243) note, though it is important to combine the activity of searching for words naturally occurring in the text with the power of working with codes, programs have usually done one or the other rather than both. There are many general database programs available on the commercial market which may be adapted to the needs of a lexical search strategy. On the other hand, programs which have been designed specifically for the use of qualitative researchers have tended to assume that analysis consists of the construction and analysis of codes and the categories that they represent. Why have qualitative analysis programs taken such a form? This is likely to be because the coding segments strategy is intended to mimic manual qualitative methods, where coded data are 'recontextualized' (Tesch, 1990), whereas lexical searching was practically impossible before the advent of concordance software.

Hypertext, too, provides a mode of organization that preserves the dynamism of data and analysis. An important reason for this is that, unlike the coding segments strategy, it does not impose a linear structure on the analytical process. This has many methodological advantages. For example, it is often argued that 'the linearization process, through which ethnographies are produced from raw data, is the primary source of cultural distortion' (White and Truex, 1988, p. 483). But, regarding the issue of flexibility of representation, hypertext promises a dynamic approach to data analysis precisely because its structure reflects that of the researcher's conceptualization of the data, and changes alongside his/her growing understanding.

Ambiguity within the coding approach

Problems surrounding the concept of coding do not appear to have been recently invented with the advent of computer tools for qualitative research, however. Richards and Richards (1991a, p. 44) note that, even in classic methodological texts, the term is problematic because it has no universal meaning. For Glaser and Strauss (1967), codes are categories which are inductive, emergent from data, and the basis upon which theory can be built. A similar view is held by Becker, Gordon and LeBailley (1984, p. 23) who argue that codes should represent categories that are based on 'common sense', rather than theory, because 'the more closely the categories are tied to a particular theory, the less useful they will be for assessing propositions put in the language of some other theory'.

By contrast, codes have a different origin and purpose for Miles and Huberman (1984). Here, codes are defined as categories which emerge from prior theory, they are more deductive than inductive, and they have the specific purpose of labelling segments of text for retrieval: 'They are *retrieval and organizing devices* that allow the analyst to spot quickly, pull out, then cluster all the segments relating to the particular question, hypothesis, concept, or theme' (1984, p. 56; emphasis in original). More simply, in Glaser and Strauss' formulation coding is a process central to the building of grounded theory, whereas in Miles and Huberman's account of qualitative analysis, coding is a means to the less creative and more mechanical end of testing theory. Whereas one is to make discoveries, the other is to test old ground rigorously.

However, applying these ideas about coding to the coding strategies adopted by available software, some writers have questioned the analytical usefulness coding for either data organization or grounded theory. For example, Christensen (1992, p. 6) notes that, while it is recognized that 'margin coding' makes diverse data more manageable, it has a disadvantage in that it does not, in itself, 'facilitate further understanding of the material. The analysis may be reduced to some kind of mechanical classification'. Here, Christensen stresses the importance of retaining a balance between mechanical classification on the one hand, and unmanageable data on the other. The problem is reconciling the goals of data organization (margin coding) and data conceptualization (open coding) - both of which are necessary in grounded theory. Seeing this as a shortcoming of existing software, he developed his own using a wordprocessor macro facility. (See Christensen, 1992, for a description of this program.)

Methodological literature on coding also reflects disagreement about the temporal position given to coding in the overall structure of data analysis. As noted by Richards and Richards (1991a, p. 50), coding or indexing is often seen as data preparation, in a 'code first, think next pattern learnt from survey research'. This approach to coding as data organization (recontextualization) is also maintained by Tesch (1991) who sees organizing activities as separate from analysis (Christensen, 1992, p. 4). By contrast, Miles and Huberman (1984) argue that the activities of coding and data organization are at the same time data analysis, since they result in a growing understanding of the phenomena under study (Christensen, 1992, p. 3). Similarly, Richards and Richards (1991a, p. 50) argue that, rather than simply preceding analysis (at which point they become a fixed object), making, shaping and exploring an index system are in themselves theorizing tasks. Thus, '[i]ndexing has to be thought of instead as a *process*, and one that goes the length of the project' (Richards and Richards, 1991a, p. 50; emphasis in original). If the latter perspective is adopted, then flexibility of the index system is vital: software must allow the researcher to change codes, items in an index, and how they are applied to text, with relative ease. This relates to an earlier point: if coding (or indexing) is the pivot of analysis, then the coding system needs to be able to accommodate the researcher's changing perceptions of the data.

Amidst confusion of the term 'coding', Richards and Richards argue that an alternative term should be used to articulate qualitative analysis which transcends and accommodates all of the variable meanings and assumptions attached to the term 'coding'. The term which they prefer, and which is used consistently in their writing about their own programNUDIST, is 'indexing'. They believe that their program offers a the first real attempt to 'combine aspects of the "grounded theory" approach with the detailed and rigourous retrieval of all text to test theory' (1991a, p. 52).

It is unlikely, however, that this confusion will be resolved simply by a general replacing of the one term with another. This is because, different ideas about coding are more to do with differences of epistemological position (regarding the construction of knowledge in qualitative analysis) than 'confusion', as such. This has implications for both the development and utilization of software for qualitative analysis. First, there is a need for various types of software which represent a diversity of coding approaches: software should not merely represent and encourage one approach at the expense of the other (Richards and Richards, 1991a, p. 50). Second, there is a need for literature accompanying software to acknowledge these differences and be explicit about their position (as have Richards and Richards) and, likewise, software consumers to be as explicit when disseminating research. This point is especially important since coding is often treated as a synonym of analysis. This conflation is problematic, not only because it excludes other approaches to analysis that do not involve coding in any shape or form, but also because there is no consistency about what coding actually means.

It seems that a systematic analysis of available software, in terms of their assumptions about the role of coding in analysis, and the extent to which they enhance or inhibit various approaches to coding, would make a significant contribution to improving the above situation. Programs for coding data do seem to share one assumption however:

> The ideas held by designers about coding do push towards more systematic and formal practical procedures. It is assumed that all data should be available to code. It is also assumed that an initial analytic hypothesis ... should be tested for confirmation/disconfirmation against all similarly coded data. The computer makes this process very thorough. (Fielding and Lee, 1991, p. 73)

These assumptions will obviously affect not only the way analysis is done, but also the types of questions and answers constructed. In particular, an analysis of the various facilities of coding software is necessary to reveal these assumptions and the way they affect analysis.

Of course, programs adopting a coding strategy vary in considerably in their specific facilities. Whereas with some programs the coding process proceeds in two steps (QUALPRO and ETHNOGRAPH), allowing the researcher to interact more thoroughly with the 'hard' data, with others coding involves only one (TAP), allowing codes to be directly entered into the computer (Tesch, 1990, p. 139). Secondly, these programs differ in terms of the number of codes which can be attached to segments, and whether overlapping or nesting of coded segments is permitted. For example, in contrast to ETHNOGRAPH, TAP does not allow more than four codes, and overlaps are not permitted. But TAP's uniqueness lies in its facility whereby the user may specify the sequence of codes to be searched (Tesch, 1990, pp. 153, 156). Thirdly, some programs (ETHNOGRAPH) have a more sophisticated facility than others (QUALPRO) for allowing the researcher to attach 'facesheet' data to text files (Tesch, 1991, pp. 34-5).

At the outset, it may be possible to distinguish between the different methodological positions of available coding software in terms of their facilities. Tesch (1990) argues that the major difference in text analysis programs is whether they focus on interpretation and description, on the one hand, or theory-building, on the other. In other words, whether they provide the technical support for the analytical procedures necessary for these different analytical goals. Both Tesch (1990), and Richards and Richards (1991a), argue that theory-building programs must be able to do three things: search for cooccurring, overlapping or nested categories; search for counterevidence to these; identify the chronological sequence of categories. It is upon the basis of these activities that the researcher is able to formulate and test hypotheses about potential relationships in the data (Walker, 1993, p. 94).

But programs vary in the extent to which they fulfil some or all of these criteria. For example, ETHNOGRAPH meets the first and second conditions in a way superior to most programs. As noted by Walker (1993, p. 95), ETHNOGRAPH 'assists in confirming hunches about the connection between categories', while its 'display of codes cooccurring with the code requested in the search command sometimes suggests connection that might not otherwise be apparent'. Other programs, do not indicate the relevance of a data segment retrieved in a particular search to other categories. In these cases, as noted by Walker (1993, p. 109), the researcher must rely entirely on his or her familiarity with data for such clues to the possible relationships between categories. However, ETHNOGRAPH does not, unlike TAP, have a specific facility for identifying sequence.

Analytical notes

Much thinking in qualitative research is done through the medium of writing notes. According to Burgess (1984), thinking-through-writing is likely to be about three things: the substantive issue at hand, the direction of analysis, and methodological issues. He also argues that each type of thinking should be deposited in memoranda designed specifically for that subject. Thus an important topic in this book is the effect various programs have on the quality and quantity of interaction with memoranda - for example, whether they have to be kept in a different database, incorporated into the same database (KWALITAN and NUDIST), or either (GUIDE) - and how this, in turn, affects analysis.

A second is the support software provides for the writing of notes into data to record 'the occasionally fleeting ideas that may eventually provide a crucial link in developing theory or interpreting meaning' (Walker, 1993, p. 95). Thus, the activity of jotting down notes would be appear essential to all programs for qualitative research, whether or not, to use Tesch's (1991) distinction, they focus on theory-building, on the one hand, or on description/interpretation, on the other. However, there is a distinct lack of facilities for this activity, as has been noted regarding ETHNOGRAPH:

> Because ... coding must be done on a printed copy of the interview and transferred to the computer, some system for tracking notes made on the printed copy has to be devised if these are to be retained and retrieved. Even if transcribed, these notes cannot be entered into the original interview without recoding the entire text (Walker, 1993, p. 108)

This problem is alleviated to some extent with the advent of the next version of ETHNOGRAPH, which allows the researcher to attach a memo of one page to any line of data (Walker, 1993, p. 108). But the degree to which it will rectify the whole problem depends upon whether there is an intrinsic difference between inserting comments into the data, or writing them elsewhere in a memo. In contrast to ETHNOGRAPH, theory-building programs support memo-writing: in an allocated place for documents (NUDIST), or in predefined theoretical and methodological memos, and 'concept cards' which are attached to data (KWALITAN). But hypertext programs, such as MARTIN (see Walker, 1993, p. 95) and GUIDE, allow the researcher to integrate notes and reflections into the data themselves, as well as attach memoranda.

Hypermedia

The meaning of 'qualitative' is generally defined negatively, as what is not 'quantitative'. Thus, qualitative research is where knowledge is based on the collection and analysis of non-numerical data. In the discourse about qualitative analysis, this definition has been largely restricted to the collection and analysis of one type of data in this category, however: text. There appears to be little explicit acknowledgement of the fact that text is but one form of representation: non-numerical data extends further than text, including graphic, audio, film, and video modes of information. Such materials are an invaluable source to modern holistic ethnography, and other traditions in qualitative research. For example film and videotape, as noted by Harper (1989), are technologies that stress holism and context which may

27

not be captured in text. However, there is a gap in methodological literature as to how such materials are integrated into computer assisted research.

Perhaps one reason for this gap is that, until recently, it was difficult to automate and integrate information that is neither numerical or textual into a computer database. Whether specifically designed for qualitative researchers or for a more general category of users, most of the software utilized by qualitative researchers are for the storage and manipulation of text. Other sources of information had to be stored and organized separately, and by manual means. Thus, the methodological discourse that has developed alongside these technological advancements has largely been devoted to examining programs exclusively designed for the analysis of text. And while authors such as Tesch (1990) may realize the narrowness of the meaning of 'qualitative' as applied in microcomputer research tools, much academic attention has been devoted to the different ways in which researchers approach words, and how various computer programs meet these needs.

Possibilities of the computer organization of information which is non-textual and non-numerical are only just beginning to be explored. One avenue which has been explored (by NUDIST) is the creation of records for non-textual data, and the indexing of this data so that it may comprehensively be included in analysis in the same way as text. But as it is 'offline', on-textual data cannot be retrieved directly. However, more exciting developments regarding computer assisted qualitative analysis of non-textual data, have coincided with the advent of hypermedia systems. These are likely to have a profound impact on qualitative research. For example, as noted by Hesse-Biber et al. (1989, p. 459) regarding their own hypermedia program which supports independent validation, '[t]he use of HYPEResearch as a methodological tool allows for important advances in the validation, reliability, and generalizability of qualitative data analysis'. Hypermedia tools offer the possibility of, not only audio and visual material being directly coded, and by different researchers, but also such materials being online for reexamination at any point in the analysis. This new technology is also likely to have a more substantive impact, as predicted by Hesse-Biber et al. (1989, p. 460), as it will 'allow the researcher to apply qualitative data analysis techniques to ever more varied and interesting phenomena'.

The remainder of this book will examine the issues raised in this chapter, alongside others thrown up by our empirical research, in relation to complementary and contrasting analytical strategies adopted by software. The first - coding segments - is the most common genre of software for qualitative analysis. The second - lexical searching - is often used in content analysis and communications research. The third chapter examines a sample of programs that fit neatly into neither a coding or lexical searching strategy because they attempt to go further than data retrieval by supporting theory-building. Finally, the discussion will focus on hypertext, the most recent genre of qualitative analysis software, which presents a novel way of approaching analysis - both of textual and non-textual data.

2 Coding segments

Introduction

As noted in the previous chapter, coding tends to be portrayed as rather straightforward, at least in literature dedicated to advocating computer-assisted analysis. It is in fact a problematic process. Coding strategies involve important assumptions and decisions which fundamentally direct data analysis. A failure to recognize the conditions and implications of those, in all their complexity, is a methodological weakness of much qualitative research. The intention of this chapter is to expose and explore the assumptions and conditions implicit to the coding method of analysis, with specific attention to the most widely used coding software: ETHNOGRAPH. However, first it is necessary to make explicit the purpose or strategy underlying coding.

The purpose of coding

The primary purpose of coding in qualitative research is the same as that in quantitative research: to structure and facilitate analysis. More specifically, coding is the strategy whereby data are segmented and tagged according to the researcher's definition of units of meaning, so that those segments which have common or related meaning can be drawn together in one place for analysis. It is in this stage of recontextualization that relations between concepts, variables and episodes can be explored and theories constructed. Thus, it is the efficient retrieval of relevant segments for recontextualization which is the main goal of the coding segments strategy.

Of course the efficiency with which we obtain this goal very much depends on the way data have been segmented and coded. One reason why this process must be treated as problematic is that it is shaped by the researcher's decisions regarding how best to facilitate the goals of data retrieval and analysis within the limits of specific software. It is anticipated that such considerations will affect both segmenting and coding respectively, and that the ways in which these problems are tackled will have profound affects on data analysis.

Some initial problems

If the data are not naturally partitioned into meaningful segments, there may be problems about knowing where to demarcate segments of text or units of analysis. According to methods guide books and manuals, the criteria with which we define segments of text are units of meaning, but what constitutes such 'units of meaning' is generally undefined or unclear. Thus, defining segments can be problematic, especially if the researcher is aware that what appears to be a unit of meaning is likely to change during the course of analysis. Working out the best way of segmenting the text is largely left up to the researcher, and this may be accomplished unconsciously or arbitrarily if one is unaware of the weight of the decision or its repercussions. It is necessary, therefore, for researchers to ask themselves certain questions before segmenting their data, in order to prepare themselves for the consequences of their actions, and maximize the sensitivity of analysis.

Similarly, devising codes is widely deemed an unproblematic activity, but there are several important questions which confront the reflective researcher. One of paramount importance, which needs to be thought about early on in the preliminary stage to coding, concerns the degree of generality or specificity that codes should represent. The way in which this question is answered will have significant effects on both coding practice and analysis of recontextualized segments. For example, if we decide to delineate a number of general, inclusive categories, much of the text will be coded with a single code (or conjunction of codes). The advantage of this strategy is that it should maximize the usefulness of codes: they are likely to be applied to enough segments to justify the purpose of recontextualization. However, it may also have several disadvantages. First, since so much text will be coded with the same category, there might be difficulty in locating particular episodes significant to analysis; a likely scenario is that the researcher will have to siphon through reams of irrelevant data, despite recontextualization. Second, coding may be too crude, and this might make the analysis seem rather vague, lacking detail, or the exploratory avenues of analysis being superficially restricted. This would be especially limiting in exploratory research, where categories and theories are completely emergent from data.

On the other hand, if we decide to define a large number of categories, with fairly exclusive meaning, the problems are reversed. Coding will be more detailed and intricate, and there will be a greater differentiation of segments accordingly. However, if the segmentation of text is too intricate, in that specific categories are attached to very small segments of text, important contextual information may be lost, and thereby some of the segments' meanings. Furthermore, it is more likely that the coding process will wind up with an exhaustive list of categories where many codes are used on only one occasion. If segments are tagged only with those codes that are later forgotten or deemed insignificant, these segments will easily become lost altogether. In addition, because coding is a linear process, some categories won't be developed until near the end of the process. This problem is intensified when using a coding scheme that consists of very specific, exclusive categories, whereas most general or thematic categories are likely to emerge relatively early on in the coding process.

Faced with this dilemma in our research, it seemed that perhaps the best solution was to devise a coding scheme that incorporated categories of various levels of generality and specificity. It was hoped that this comprehensive approach would offset the disadvantages, while retaining the advantages, of each coding strategy. (And, in the context of the distinctively methodological focus of our study, it would also provide the opportunity to explore the methodological consequences of each strategy upon analysis.) This decision formed the principle of the preliminary coding scheme or 'organizing system' (Tesch, 1990). The next two sections explain the scheme in more detail; first in principle, and then how it worked in practice.

The coding scheme: in principle

Method of development

Before the coding process can begin (i.e. the text is segmented and codes are assigned to segments), an organizing system or provisional set of categories must be designed. As noted in the previous section, this task is by no means unproblematic: even deciding on a basic rationale can be riddled with methodological questions. This is particularly the case in much interpretive qualitative research (or open-ended questions in social surveys), where the coding scheme is not derived from a theoretical framework, or from substantive questions guiding the research. Instead, it has to be constructed from the data themselves, and its development is largely ongoing with coding rather then being prior to it. Since there seems to be commonsense or correct way of developing a rationale for coding, 'individual researchers have different "recipes"' for doing this (Tesch, 1990, p. 91). From our experience, careful consideration of the degree of generality or detail required from the analysis, and the consequences of moving from one level of abstraction to another, must form an important part of this decision.

In our research, we began to build the coding scheme and a rationale for its organization, by drawing out themes from the first three days of fieldnotes, and generally 'getting a feel' for the data. Thus, the codes that emerged in this process reflected topics to which the segments were relevant, rather than summarizing their particular content, such as particular characteristics of the field setting. Ideas and questions about the dimensions of themes, and the interrelations between these dimensions and other themes, were noted in 'analytic memoranda'. Upon this basis, a skeletal coding paradigm was developed, with which data could be systematically coded; we also believed that the system was flexible enough to accommodate any necessary modifications.

Rationale

The organizing system basically consisted of two layers. The first layer was essentially made up of conceptual codes in the context of formal, abstract theory, and were thus necessarily general and inclusive. Much of the text would be segmented according to such codes. The second layer, on the other hand, was constituted from empirical codes which represented specific substantive topics (which, although recurring, would not be used as widely as the more abstract codes), and significant features of the subject of study, which are even more exclusive. The organizing system can be represented by the following diagram (figure 2.1), where various types of codes occupy different positions on a continuum:

THEORETICAL POSITION OF CODE		GENRE OF CODE
abstract/conceptual/general	↑	thematic
		topic
		cast
concrete/empirical/specific	↓	episodic

Figure 2.1   The coding scheme. This consists of several genres of codes (on the right), each of which implies a different level of theoretical abstraction (on the left).

The idea behind the coding scheme was that it would be broad enough to incorporate various types of categories. This is because, as indicated earlier, it is difficult to determine, at the outset of analysis, how general or specific categories should be. Moreover, we believe that it is desirable for researchers to be able to work with a diversity of codes in this respect. More specifically, researchers should be able to combine codes of various degrees of abstraction, and have the freedom to move from one level of abstraction to another (from general to specific and from specific to general). For this purpose, explicit distinctions were drawn between general and specific codes to facilitate awareness of the direction an analytical path is taking. This helps the researcher to be reflexive about analytical decisions, and the consequences that their analytical paths entail.

i) Thematic codes Themes are the most general and abstract categories. They tend to run throughout sociological discourse as a whole, rather than being limited to the substantive field in question. Themes (such as gossip, divisions of labour, and social control) are abstract and conceptual, and knowledge

34

about them primarily derives from sociological discourse rather than from the empirical data at hand. When these themes are located in data, they are often done so with respect of a certain dimension. For example, this may be concerning the particular person involved (gossip about Walters), the classes of persons involved (division of labour between nursing shifts; inter-departmental division of labour), or the particular aspect of a more general phenomenon (formal/institutional mechanisms of patient control; informal/individual strategies of patient control).

Ideally, codewords will reflect these various dimensions, as well as the general theme. This could be achieved in several ways. The first strategy would be to use letter cases systematically to distinguish between the two: upper case letters for general themes (DOL for division of labour), followed by lower case letters to depict a specific dimension (DOLshift). Other ways of organizing thematic codewords are to use a slash between its two parts (DOL/SHIFT) or a number (0506) which corresponds to an index of categories (the sixth dimension of the fifth theme in the list). If this is achieved it may be possible, in the data retrieval stage, to search for both a theme as a whole and one of its dimensions, from a single codeword.

ii) topic codes This is a very broad class of codes, including variables (gender; ethnicity; age; class; education), strategies (attention-seeking; instrumentalism; formality; authority; patient indulgence; punishment; solidarity; safety; hygiene), conditions (confinement; visiting; supervision; medical health; training; medical equipment), and consequences (violence; conflict; trust; sympathy; institutional dependence). This is a broad class of codes because many codes fit into more than one of the above categories (violence and confinement may be strategies, conditions or consequences in various contexts) so it seemed inappropriate to divide them into smaller groups.

Although some topic codes will reflect standard social variables, and others may represent policy issues, for example, categories generally are rooted much more in the data than are thematic ones. Since they are emergent categories, their number will continue to increase throughout the coding process. The fact that this list can continue to increase is important since it enables a more open and detailed coding of data. Also, since many of these categories signify topics which cross-cut themes, they may be applied independently rather than being tied to specific themes.

iii) Cast codes These categories are completely exclusive to and emergent from the data: the participants in the field. They are also very specific and are defined with relative ease. It was decided that, in addition to thematic and topic codes, data should also be coded in respect of whose actions are being described or views expressed as this may be useful in the data retrieval stage. This was for several reasons. For example, when exploring the relation between fear of contamination and technical knowledge of the disease, we may want to retrieve the actions and views of a particular

35

attendant (Walters), if familiarity with data through coding had suggested such a relation.

It was also decided that cast codewords should identify, not only the name of each character, but also include the rank of each character (AT/WALTERS). This would encourage characters to be seen in terms of their roles and positions in the social hierarchy. Since roles depict institutionalized patterns, these indicators will help draw attention beyond the personal characteristics of individuals to the setting as a whole, so that acts and actors may be perceived in their social context.

These codes are important for several reasons. First, knowing people's identities, and their position within social relations, can have various effects on the nature of accounts they produce, because they determine the channels of information and filters of understanding available to those people. Furthermore, 'the interpretation of information available to a person is likely to be selected and slanted in line with his or her prevailing concerns' (Hammersley and Atkinson, 1983, p. 194). This renders two possible uses of ranked cast codes. First, they may be useful for the methodological purpose of keeping bias in check. Alternatively, where the explicit aim of analysis is to explore how social location shapes accounts of reality, or the contextuality of meanings, they may be a source of enlightenment and a powerful analytical tool.

For example, by conducting a multiple search on AT/WALTERS and CONTAM, and comparing it to similar multiple searches on other attendants and CONTAM, we can explore the ideas about contamination characteristic of this particular occupational group, and the factors that affect these ideas. Similarly, a combined search on AT/WALTERS, DR/DAY, and HYG will retrieve all interactions where hygiene is at issue and both of these characters are involved. In this way, the views and actions of one actor, regarding a particular issue, may be contrasted with those of an actor of a different position.

Finally, in order to examine more general roles and institutional contexts in more detail, separate categories were also devised for the more generic institutional position of actors (as opposed to their more specific rank). Thus, whereas cast codes differentiate between charge nurses (CN/FARRELL), registered nurses (RN/HODGE), and practical nurses (PN/HILLYER), there is in addition the general category NURSE. This would enable researchers to work on a more general level and systematically to search for and compare the social attributes of one class, such as nurses, with those of another, such as attendants. These two types of cast codes - actor specific and occupation specific - will be concurrently applied to the data.

iv) Episodic codes These categories are completely exclusive to the data at hand. Moreover, they are exclusive to a particular point in the data. Episodic codes are not therefore designed for the purposes of recontextualization (as they never appear more than once in the text), but they will aid the development of concepts and theories at the level of the general and more abstract.

During the initial reading of the data, we noticed that there were several episodes which constituted significant units of analysis because they drew together various themes, or demonstrated the relation between topics or variables. For example, take the following segment of fieldnotes:

> At one time, Hodge told me, the exercise patients had been allowed to line up at the tray cart and receive their trays. However, one 80 year old man brushed against the tray cart and the people in the kitchen let out a howl about the patients contaminating their cart. They demanded that the trays be carried to the patients so that the patients could not come near the cart and that has been done since then. Both Hodge and Bailey thought this was silly and that the people in the kitchen were unnecessarily sensitive about the possibility of contamination. (This is a very common sort of conflict in a TB hospital. Those who have a great deal of contact with patients tend to lose their fear of catching the disease, while those who don't have direct contact with the patients consider TB much more dangerous and much more easily caught than is actually the case. Therefore, those working on the ward such as the kitchen help are too fearful, while those not working closely with the patients consider the ward personnel too careless.)

This segment was coded EP/TROLLEY because it illustrates an episode which crystallizes interdepartmental conflict regarding attitudes to contamination in a particularly powerful way. Also it captures analytical commentary which relates this specific episode to a more general phenomenon (identified by Roth in the fieldnotes as the inverse relation between the degree of contact with patients, and the degree of fear of contamination). Thus it was anticipated that the segment would serve as a good example or illustrative material when examining such general phenomena, and therefore needed to be easily accessible.

As the above extract illustrates, the analytic usefulness of episodes lies in their ability to illuminate local interpretative meaning dramatically and serve as a powerful insight to actors' definitions and social processes. Since they are high on imagery, they tend to stick in the minds of researchers, and thus may be remembered when examining a particular idea. The very fact that an episode is suddenly remembered in a certain connection deserves its instant retrieval, and this is made possible by the fact that it has been coded.

Having described the rationale or organizing system for our coding scheme, the next section will turn to the consequences of this design: the decisions, actions and processes that arising from its application to the task of coding, and its tailoring to the particular needs of ETHNOGRAPH.

The coding scheme: in practice

Contextual meaning

Another ongoing problem throughout the coding process is knowing how much contextual information to include in a segment. This is even problematic where categories very exclusive. For example, although only text relevant to a particular patient, Linn, can be coded P/LINN, how do we define the boundaries of what is relevant to that category? Is it what Linn does in particular, or the whole context of his action?

Similarly, this problem occurs regarding topics. In the following extract for example, should it be only the last sentence that is tagged with RELIGION, or the whole section?

> Lovell, Freund and Hodge were discussing a young woman named Donna Clemens on A Ward. Donna apparently is quite ill and has been for a long time. She is somebody who is very appreciative of the care she's getting and they all like her very much and try to do things for her but at the same time are afraid that she's not doing well physically. She seems quite fearful according to Bailey, and wants to have somebody with her all the time. She's always trying to think of reasons for getting people to come in and see her and talk to her. Mrs Nesbitt, the occupational therapist, said she spent two hours with her yesterday reading portions of the bible to her and that seemed to calm her down somewhat.

It is only in terms of the first part of the extract that religious need is given a context. Without reading the events occurring before the sentence of interest, we would not know that the topic arises in a nurses' discussion of Donna's attention-seeking behaviour, which is associated with her fear of a deteriorating medical condition. It is only in terms of the whole section that bible-reading emerges as attention-seeking behaviour (in the nurses' interpretation), rather than an expression of religious need: it is the attention gained through this activity that is comforting to Donna, not the Bible's words themselves. Furthermore, we would not know that this interpretation is not necessarily shared by Bailey and Mrs Nesbitt, despite the appearance of their statements in the extract. For they are not present in this encounter: their stories are rewritten and given new meaning in a conversation between a group of nurses.

The point is that a segment's context is always important, especially if the segment is quite small and constitutes only part of a paragraph. Obviously, there would be no point in coding at all if all context needed to be taken into account. But reflection about the amount of context to include in a segment, and whether the segment's meaning alters considerably when it is decontextualized (extracted from its original fieldnote context), is certainly necessary when coding the data. Possible implications for later stages of analysis always need careful consideration during the coding process.

In our research, these considerations produced an increasing tendency to define whole paragraphs as segments, rather than the smaller items within them. This method may entail another danger however: the researcher will be confronted with much more text as a result of a search, which may stifle the analytical focus or creativity of the researcher, or simply prove frustrating when trying to locate items of interest in large paragraphs.

Nested and overlapping segments

Of course, with ETHNOGRAPH, one paragraph does not have to be defined as only one segment: it may be divided into several levels of nested and overlapping segments. Overlapping segments share one or more lines of data, whereas nested segments are those which are completely contained within a larger segment. Taking this facility of ETHNOGRAPH into account when coding was not problematic in itself. Indeed, it seemed common sense to code data in this way, given our coding scheme. For often a whole paragraph is relevant to a certain theme, and therefore defined as a segment, but this paragraph also contains bits of data that are relevant to other types of category, such as topics. These 'bits' of data are all smaller than the paragraph, but their sizes and positions also vary, forming several nests and overlapping segments within the paragraph. We anticipated that this facility would be an asset later on in analysis.

However, despite feeling 'natural' at the time, it seemed that approaching the data in this way was an effect of ETHNOGRAPH's facilities for overlaps and nests. It was because we knew the program accommodated a complex organization of segments, that we began the coding the data in this way. It was not until later in the coding process that we questioned this way of seeing the data, and considered that a simpler method of disaggregating the data may be more practical. These questions arose for several reasons.

First, despite the program's facility for nests and overlaps, and that this actively encouraged categorizing the data in such terms, these goals were continually frustrated during coding: we continually found ourselves running up against limits, imposed by ETHNOGRAPH, regarding the number of overlapping and nested segments permitted (figure 2.2). The fact that a single line of text cannot belong to any more than seven different segments made coding often seem inadequate for indicating the data's relevance to the appropriate range of analytical categories.

Solutions to this problem usually consisted of a juggling act, whereby we tried to avoid the ETHNOGRAPH's restrictions by adjusting segment boundaries until the program would accept it (figure 2.3). However, this brings into play a new set of problems. For example, the solution shown in the figure below risks the loss of important contextual information: if a multiple search is conducted on codes 'a AND i' (i.e. where these two codes have both been applied to the same lines of text), only lines 7 to 12 will be retrieved, thus losing the contextual information contained in lines 1 to 6. This kind of outcome must always be borne in mind when deciding how best to accommodate the limitations of coding software during coding.

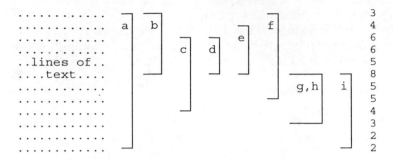

Figure 2.2 **A common problem encountered when coding was that we wanted to assign one segment of text to more than seven segments (as indicated by the numbers on the far right of the diagram) which is in excess of ETHNOGRAPH's limits for nests and overlaps.**

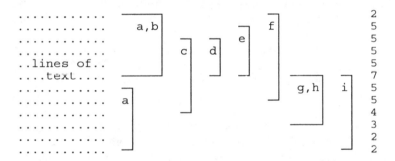

Figure 2.3 **A solution: one segment (a) is divided into two (where a new sentence begins), allowing its upper half to become equal to another segment (b) so that they can be counted as one (a,b). Thus, there is no longer any line of text belonging to more than seven segments.**

In addition to the problems generated by ETHNOGRAPH's technical restrictions, a second consideration brought into question the extensive definition of nested and overlapping segments. This is related to the problems set out in the previous section regarding contextual meaning. It soon became clear that, in some situations, there will be no opportunity to view the external levels of a nest, or the external parts of an overlap, when they are retrieved later in analysis. For not only are we unable to browse around a retrieved segment, but we are not always given the option of taking a 'big view' of nests and overlaps: while being available for 'multiple searches', this option is unavailable for instances where data are searched using only one code.

It is not clear why ETHNOGRAPH should grant the opportunity to see external nests and overlaps in multiple searches but not in single ones. But it seems to reflect an assumption about the nature of analysis: it is only when theorizing about and testing the relations between categories that we need to be interested in external segments. For example, if one category is continually contained within another, this may suggest that the former is related to a specific dimension of the latter. In this context, a 'big view' of nests and overlaps in a single search is assumed unnecessary, because this type of search is designed for the exploration and articulation of a specific category. However, this assumption is unfounded and potentially very limiting, because the development of a category is not achieved in isolation, but rather in terms of its relation to others. This does not mean that single searches should simply be abandoned, since multiple searches imply specifying other categories, and researchers are often not in the position to do this early on in analysis. In short, this limitation of ETHNOGRAPH seems to stifle types of analytic induction. Since this seems to be the whole point of recontextualizing data in terms of a single category, the single search facility is somewhat redundant.

In any case, becoming aware of this shortcoming of ETHNOGRAPH regarding single searches had an impact on outstanding coding. For we did not want to place ourselves in a situation where we were unable to examine a segment's wider context if desired. Thus we had to reconsider our approach to defining segments. More specifically, we had to override the tendency to use nests and overlaps extensively, and instead use a simpler, more inclusive approach. Again, the effect was that whole paragraphs tended to be defined as a segment, with all codes attached to this segment rather than the smaller items within it.

Too many codes?

When applying the coding system to the data, on several occasions we found that a segment required more than twelve codes, but this number exceeded the capabilities of ETHNOGRAPH. It is likely that this was due largely to inefficiency regarding the use of 'cast codes' and the fact that these were used to depict not only each character, but also their generic occupational group. A segment capturing an interaction between three actors of different status was tagged, in line with our coding strategy, with six cast codes (AT/BECKER, RN/HUDSON, DR/MCLEAN, ATT, NURSE, DR) thus using up half of ETHNOGRAPH's limit even before the application of any other types of codes accounting for themes, topics and episodes.

It seemed that, because of the program's requirements, a more exclusive rule of using these codes would be necessary. One method of doing this is to minimize potentially meaningless multiple coding: not all cast codes applied to a segment will be useful. Thus ETHNOGRAPH makes demands on researchers to be more discerning in the application of cast codes: a character's appearance in the fieldnotes need be coded only if his/her role is deemed significant, instead of every time a character is mentioned.

Thus we decided to use name codes (AT/HAYWARD; PN/LEWIS) only if the identity of a particular actor is significant and, similarly, status codes (att; nurse; kitchen) only if the class of actor is significant. This approach renders the coding process less mechanical, and should hopefully make the process of coding the data within the requirements of ETHNOGRAPH more manageable. However, by the same token, it also makes coding more problematic: there is always the fear that these judgements are prematureor unfounded in such an early stage of data interpretation, and that potentially important data will thereby be lost because they are not appreciated as such in the coding process.

Actors - present or absent?

When designing the organizing system at the outset of coding, we decided that two types of cast codes would be used to capture the specific identity and occupational status of actors. However, it soon became apparent that a third type of cast code was necessary. This is because characters may appear in the text in two ways: either directly (by actively participating in contemporary action) or indirectly (by being talked about). We have already seen some of the problems that can emerge due to ambiguity about present and absent actors in the extract about Donna's attention-seeking. However, the coding system did not initially recognize this differentiation and so needed updating. Thus, special categories were devised to account for those instances where a character is the subject of conversation or gossip. The codewords for these cast codes are differentiated from the others by the prefix (signifying 'gossip') which is followed by the name of the person subject to gossip.

Of course, codes that differentiate between present and absent actors not only help clarify interpretation, but also enable the retrieval of all bits of data where a particular person is the subject of gossip, and even specify the persons participating in that gossip. Say we were interested in the various representations. We already know from coding the data that a particular patient (Linn) is often portrayed as violent and aggressive, especially by a certain attendant (Walters). Thus our analytic goal can be given an initial focus by conducting a multiple search using the gossip code for Linn (GOSS/LINN), the standard cast code for Walters (AT/WALTERS), and the topic code for violence (VIOLENCE).

However, careful judgement must again be used to decide when to apply the GOSS code: there will be many passing comments made about characters which are not significant and which do not, therefore, need to be coded.

Our organizing system consisted of several code sets (thematic, episodic etc), and each set contained a large number of individual codes. This proved to be problematic for coding because it is impossible to be sensitive to a large number of categories all at once when coding a piece of text. On the other hand, if codes are overlooked in the coding process, and the relevance of pieces of data to those categories is not recognized, this can have important consequences for construct validity. The risk is that analysis, and therefore theorizing, will not strictly be grounded in the data. At the very least, the development of categories and concepts during recontextualization will be impaired, because not all data relevant to them will be retrieved in a search. And, as we shall see, these consequences are not merely for those categories underrepresented in coded data.

Categories are not developed in isolation, but in terms of their relations with other categories. Thus, the connections between related categories may also fail to be sufficiently explored as a result of sloppy coding. For if a category had been applied to data more thoroughly, its retrieval in a search may have had something new to say about other categories, even those that would have otherwise remained absolutely unrelated, or irrelevant. Thus, possible avenues of analysis and theory-building may be blocked to some extent if data are not coded in terms of all categories.

Lack of systematicity in the assignment of categories to data is especially problematic in early analysis, given the maxim of open coding. According to Strauss (1987, p. 28), open coding is the initial, unrestricted coding of data 'to open up the enquiry'. Researchers are urged to code inclusively and 'wildly': anything that might be relevant to a given category - no matter how remote - should be coded (Lofland, 1971; Hammersley and Atkinson, 1983). This is because analysis proceeds in the manner of 'funnelling' (Dey, 1993) or 'progressive focusing' (Hammersley and Atkinson, 1983). In this context, it is better to find that some irrelevant data are retrieved in a search than not finding all relevant data.

However, it also has important consequences for later stages of analysis, or when there is a fine-grained coding of data, especially in theory-building research. For if data are not systematically coded in terms of all variables, then the construction of propositions will be grounded only in parts of the data, and the testing of propositions (through searching for combinations of codes) will be inaccurate. For example, say we wanted to test the following hypothesis: 'differing practices of isolation techniques not only reflect varying models of contamination, but also constitute strategies for reaffirming cultural difference'. Our testing of this hypothesis, in terms of searching for confirming and disconfirming evidence, would be meaningless unless all the codes for various social and cultural differences, as well as those for isolation technique and contamination, had been considered for all data. But even having recognized the problem of systematicity, there is no straightforward solution.

Dey (1993, p. 119) has noted that to be systematic about coding requires 'considerable concentration, in order to ensure that all the appropriate categories for all the data have been considered' Since the problem is due to spreading attention over a long list of categories, many of which are irrelevant, he argues that the situation can be improved if the list is first pruned down to 'likely prospects and possibilities' (Dey, 1993, p. 122). However, it remains unclear how one should work out what these actually are. Similarly, Tesch (1990, p. 123) makes the useful point that, while most researchers 'extract all relevant segments from one data document at a time, coding them into the categories as they go along' (rather than focusing on one category at a time), this is not the only possible approach. But, again the consequences of these strategies for systematicity are not made explicit.

For example, scrutinizing a piece of text (say, a paragraph), with reference to every item on the coding scheme before it is coded, will ensure that categories are not forgotten while coding. But those codes assumed irrelevant will still largely be skipped. The other approach is 'axial coding' (Strauss, 1987), where data are analyzed in terms of, or coded along the axis of, one category at a time. This strategy has the advantage of focusing on one category throughout the span of the data as a whole, and thus is likely to further its cumulative development as a concept, as well as its accurate application to data. But the opposite temptation, of skipping over those data that seem to be obviously irrelevant. Furthermore, the gains of these strategies in making coding more systematic need to be weighed against their costs: both make coding a much longer, more laborious process, than the original strategy of coding for whatever category comes to mind.

Defining codes

During coding, it became increasingly necessary for the meaning of categories to be explicitly defined. This is because, as categories became more complicated both quantitatively (in number) and qualitatively (in meaning), it became more difficult to differentiate between categorys in order to decide which category was suitable for a particular piece of text.

For example, take the following extract from the fieldnotes:

> It looks as though the research on the transmission of tuberculosis which has been done in recent years has made practically no impression on the procedure of the nursing department.

On our list of categories, we have EDUCATION and TRAINING, but by simply knowing the codewords for these categories, it is not immediately clear which one we should assign to the segment, or whether we should assign both or neither.

Although we had some idea of each category's meaning when initially naming them, this meaning was largely implicit or taken for granted as self-explanatory. This may be for two reasons. First, category meanings were unconsciously defined by commonsense or sociological meanings implicitly associated with the name of the category. Second, category meanings seem self-explanatory because they are context-dependent: their meaning is obvious in terms of the context in which they were constructed. However, both of these conditions change during analysis, as we associate different meanings to codewords and move further away from original contexts.

Thus it is necessary for researchers to define what each category means as they are created, drawing upon knowledge of the data so far coded and 'experiential data', and record this definition for future reference. When this is the case, we locate the meanings of training and education by looking in the appropriate analytic memos (figure 2.4).

analytic memo provisional category definition EDUCATION This category refers to views about the nature of disease, and where they are situated in relation to various 'lay' and 'expert' knowledges. It is expected that these will depend largely upon the occupational status of actors, since such roles entail various types of socialization. In contrast to TRAINING, it is concerned with concrete rules and practices only as far as they reveal models of knowledge about disease and contamination.	analytic memo provisional category definition TRAINING This category focuses on the technical knowledge required by staff to execute their roles in the division of labour effectively. This may range from managing medical equipment to being sensitive to the needs of patients. It is only used when the ability of staff in these respects is questioned or commented upon, unlike EDUCATION which focuses more specifically on the medical knowledge that such practices entail.

Figure 2.4 Analytic memoranda containing definitions for categories. These memos support the coding process and are designed to reflect the state of development of a category. This figure contains provisional working definitions (i.e. those created at the time the categories were created) for the codes EDUCATION and TRAINING.

Furthermore, the coding process should be occasionally interrupted so that existing definitions of categories may be further refined and elaborated. This practice, albeit one not explicitly encouraged by ETHNOGRAPH, facilitates a more accurate coding of data.

In addition, defining codes in such an explicit and elaborate fashion enables researchers tentatively to explore relations between categories (such as between training and education, and the relation of both to the division of labour) because categories are necessarily defined in relation to other categories. Thus code definitions are useful, not only for the process of coding the data, but also as guides to the next level of analysis; the process of defining and elaborating triggers the asking of questions, development of propositions, and pondering of theoretical possibilities.

However, defining categories is more easily said than done. In much qualitative research, almost all knowledge, propositions, and questions are emergent from thinking about the data. Thus TRAINING cannot satisfactorily be defined until a substantial amount of data have been coded with it (according to its preliminary working definition). It is only then that the category becomes more meaningful and refined. This means that coding requires not only the explicit definition of categories at the time of their conception, but also their continual redefinition.

The process of refining the definitions of categories is also complicated by another feature of qualitative analysis: concepts and topics have varying rates of development, largely due to their irregular appearance chronologically in the data. Some categories emerge as themes early on in the data and are therefore available for more detailed development, whereas others may emerge only in the last few pages of fieldnotes and thus develop much later. Indeed, their 'saturation' (Glaser and Strauss, 1967) is unlikely to be reached at all without a recoding of all data preceding the conceptualization of those categories.

Refining code definitions

As the meanings attached to codes become more sophisticated, and changes in conceptualization are explicitly documented in analytic memoranda, the application of these codes to data also needs to be modified. But this, of course, is a very difficult task, especially if such categories have already been used extensively to code data. This is because modifications of category definitions changes the relevance of that code for data. First, the code may no longer be relevant to all the segments previously assigned to it. Second, it may require the segments to which it has been applied to be defined in a different way; the updated code may be relevant to more text around the segment (demanding the segment to be enlarged), or only to smaller items within the segment (demanding the segment to be reduced in size).

To go back to the previous example, say much of the data had already assigned with the code TRAINING, using the definition shown in figure 2.4. However, somewhere in the middle of the coding process, we added the following clause to the code's definition:

> Rather than focusing on the types of knowledge that are required, this category depicts the amount of emphasis given to certain activities in the training of new staff (i.e Roth). This should indicate those practices which are considered to be difficult (demanding much skill or practice) or important, as compared with those which are taken for granted or considered to be of little value.

This clause has, in effect, made the category more exclusive. Thus, not all those segments that were coded with TRAINING with reference to its more inclusive meaning (see figure 2.4) will be relevant to the updated category. We will therefore need to read all data again in terms of this new definition, in order to code for the category accurately.

Thus, in short, the fact that the definitions of categories are largely contingent upon those of others, along with the fact that categories have different rates of development, proves to be problematic for the coding segments strategy. More simply, it is the dynamic relations between categories, and the fact that they are contingent on particular ways of interacting with the data, or moments in analysis which change the way we think about something, which this strategy finds difficult to accommodate.

Perhaps the best way to reduce this problem is to develop an intricate system of categories, as a result of a detailed preliminary analysis of the data as a whole, before coding any of the data properly. However, this is likely to postpone rather than transcend the problem. For even if it avoids the problem in the coding stage, the researcher will, at some point in analysis (if any good), propose new concepts and relations which will affect old categories. From this perspective, it would seem that the question of when to start coding the data with a set of categories becomes the essential, but impossible, question to answer.

Coding for specific aspects of topics

Broadly speaking, all categories are variables in the sense that they can either be relevant to (or present in) the data, or else irrelevant to (or absent in) the data. Some topics in our coding scheme (autoclave; staff breaks; alcohol use; face mask), like cast codes, are variables in this sense only. Thus deciding whether or not to apply these topic codes to data is fairly straightforward. However, topic codes are a heterogeneous collection of categories which, in addition to material conditions and objects, include specific concepts, attitudes, strategies, mechanisms, and consequences (education; approachability; dependence; competence; flexibility; training). These types of codes are conceptual, abstract, and inherently social: since they are not material and concrete, they cannot simply be classified as either present or absent in data. The status of 'flexibility' as a variable, and knowing when or when not to apply it to data, is much more ambiguous and complex than is 'autoclave' (a particular piece of sterilizing equipment).

When we were coding the data, it soon emerged that the codes for these more complex topics needed to be reconceptualized. For the codes we had previously devised to represent phenomena, implied a focus on only one of their aspects. For example, TRAINING is assigned to segments which indicate actors' views about certain tasks requiring trained staff, in that they are important or demand particular skills, so that they need to be taught rather than learned through experience. But what if hospital staff express a view about a particular task being mundane or unimportant? Do we attach the TRAINING code or not? We obviously do not want to lose these views, because ideas about mundane and pointless work form part of the context in which other tasks are constructed as important or difficult. Yet, on the other hand, it seems insufficient to code the segment with the code as it stands,

47

because the data capture the inverse or negative of training, as it were: special training is not required for the task at hand.

Once this was recognized, it seemed natural to incorporate into our coding scheme codes which, instead of simply depicting the presence of a concept or variable, also depict the value of that concept or variable in a particular instance. The value of a variable is represented by the suffix '+' or '-' appearing at the end of the codeword. Thus one concept (flexibility) has two codes (FLEX+ and FLEX-), which respectively depict whether the concept's positive value (flexibility) or negative value (inflexibility) is relevant to the text in question. This tactic should, in principle, have several advantages in the data retrieval stage of analysis. First, it should enable a 'single search' on a specific value of a variable (either its positive or negative instance), allowing all segments related to this value or dimension to be set together in one place for comparison. Second, it should enable a 'multiple search' on a variable or concept in general (both of its values), allowing all data relevant to an entire concept or topic to be recontextualized for further analysis.

The ability to move between both of these possibilities in data retrieval and analysis is important. By specifying the values of variables in a search, we may be more able to see relations otherwise blurred by, or buried in, more general codes. This practice is essentially the same as that described as 'splitting variables' by Miles and Huberman (1984, p. 222), which is a useful tactic for 'finding coherent, integrated descriptions and explanations', and for avoiding 'monolithism and blurring of data'. However, it is also important that these differentiations can be ignored, if so desired (a search for the category 'flexibility' in general can be achieved by searching for both FLEX+ and FLEX-). According to the principles of generating meaning set out by Miles and Huberman (1984), one tactic is to subsume the particulars under the general, moving to constructs and then to theories, in order to establish 'more-than-one-study propositions that account for the"how" and "why" of phenomena'. Finally, the fact that this strategy enables researchers to follow either direction was seen as one its merits: it enables a flexible approach to analysis. This is because types of recontextualization and the theoretical development of categories are not restricted by codes being either too specific or too general.

Coding for topics in general

However, this strategy seems to be somewhat disappointing in practice (at least in context of our particular coding software), for it is not always possible to be systematic about coding for a particular aspect of a category. This seems to be rooted in the variability in data, because they do not necessarily express specific aspects of topics at all. In many cases, data express the topic as a whole, or its relation to others, without mentioning specifics. In other cases, the data express both: a segment often begins with a statement about a general phenomenon, and then illustrates the point by focusing on a specific dimension of the phenomenon (or vice versa). This proves to be a problem for the coding process when there are only value-specific categories for topics (or dimension-specific categories for themes). And even if we use more general categories, this introduces different problems into coding. These problems will now be examined more fully in relation to an example.

Take the following extract from the fieldnotes:

> The attendants are willing to help each other out if one gets ahead of the other because it is all, so to speak, in the family. Even the nurses will help the attendants to some extent as Hodge did me today because this again is within the nursing department and they are helping out their own people even though they are people at a somewhat lower level. The maintenance workers, however, are in an entirely different department and are regarded as outsiders.

This segment indicates a relationship between the degree of flexibility in formal work roles, on the one hand, and the type of division of labour, on the other. It also seems that 'sense of community' is an intervening variable. This association may be stated in the form of two hypotheses:

- Division of labour within departments is conducive to a community atmosphere' and a flexible attitude to formal roles
- Division of labour between departments is a source of competition and roles in this context remain strictly separate and inflexible

These propositions may later be tested by searching for confirming and disconfirming evidence. But first the segment needs to be appropriately coded, and this is where difficulty arises.

The section of fieldnotes can be approached from at least two levels. First, it may be approached on a microscopic level so that all specifics of the situation (division of labour between departments; division of labour between attendants and nurses; division of labour between nursing and maintenance staff; community; flexibility; inflexibility) are coded. But the segment also suggests that there is a causal relation between these categories at a more general or abstract level. Thus, coding may also be approached on a macroscopic level, so that categories in their most general form (division of labour; community; flexibility) are coded. It seemed to us that both ways of looking at the data needed to be represented in the way it was coded, and thus it suddenly became apparent that the ability to subsume the particulars under the general was not only limited to the retrieval stage: general phenomena also have to be represented in coded data.

Yet how can this be achieved? General codes, such as flexibility, had previously been abandoned in favour of codes that were value-specific. Thus, if we want to stick with this decision, the segment will need to be coded with both FLEX+ and FLEX- in order to signify its relevance to the category as a whole. The segment will then be retrieved in a single search for either value, or a multiple search for both values and thereby the category in general. However, this technique of denoting the relevance of general categories implies a method of 'double coding'. Double coding can be problematic if there are more than a few topic codes assigned to the data. For by the time cast and thematic codes are added, ETHNOGRAPH's maximum of twelve codes per line of text may soon become insufficient.

Alternatively, we could account for general topics (or themes), by turning a full circle and reintroducing general codes (without the '+' or '-' suffix) into the coding scheme. These codes will denote nothing of a variable's value or dimension at a particular instance - merely its presence as a variable. These general codes (FLEX) could be used in addition to value or dimension specific codes (FLEX+; FLEX-) to denote the presence of a variable as a whole (or its presence in a state of neutrality). This provides a solution to the problem of double-coding when a variable has no specific value or dimension, but not when we want to code for both specific values and general categories; there is a need to use general categories to be assigned in conjunction with specific ones, because the data segment describes instances where staff are flexible, and where they are inflexible, as well as being relevant to the topic 'flexibility' in general. Thus, in this case, rather than solving the problem of double coding, having a general code as well as specific codes for a category introduces problems of triple coding (FLEX, FLEX+, FLEX-). It seems that the only way this can be solved is to abandon value specific categories altogether.

Thus here is the dilemma in short: during coding, it seems necessary to make a commitment to sacrifice either specificity for generality on the one hand, generality for specificity on the other or, if a compromise is sought, run into the technical problems of exceeding ETHNOGRAPH's code limit. The necessity for this kind of decision is exclusive to the coding strategy of data analysis, and the only guidance available to researchers making this decision is the purpose of their research, and the kinds of questions they want to ask. Since the goals of our research were exclusively methodological, we wanted to keep as many analytical avenues open as possible. Thus value-specific categories were retained, and it was hoped that the hazards of double coding (for a variable's general and undifferentiated form) would be not be encountered very often.

Coding - a dynamic or static process?

In sum, coding data is a problematic process, requiring researchers to make all kinds of decisions, and be reflective about their implications. In other words, it is necessary continually to project forwards to later stages of analysis (as well as backwards to earlier coding tactics), in order to apply codes to the text in the most efficient way; it is necessary to keep in mind the conditions in which the segment will and will not be retrieved, in order to maximize the retrieval of wanted information and minimize the retrieval of unwanted information during searches. A balance must be achieved between two types of problems related to, both, the application of codes, and the definition of boundaries. First, codes must be accurately applied to the data to avoid the retrieval of too many irrelevant segments of text, on the one hand, and losing relevant segments, on the other. Second, boundaries must be accurately defined in order to avoid the retrieval of too much irrelevant contextual information, on the one hand, and not enough that is relevant, on the other. Thus researchers have to be aware of four potential hazards when coding the data, all of which may impede theoretical development.

This point concerns the efficiency rather than the methodology of the coding strategy. It is still important, however. It is because of their supposed 'efficiency' and identity as 'research tools' that software such as ETHNOGRAPH justify their existence. If reaching their potential to facilitate analysis involves a long and troublesome process of data preparation, microcomputing strategies may actually have more disadvantages than advantages. If researchers are not careful when coding, analysis is likely to be impeded, whereas if every decision is carefully considered (and there are a lot of decisions to be made), there is still the nagging chance that something has been forgotten or overlooked and exploratory paths unwittingly closed. Indeed it is precisely the flexible, cumulative and unpredictable character of ethnographic analysis which proves to be so problematic for the process of coding data.

Ethnography is a flexible and eclectic approach to data collection:

> Since it does not entail extensive pre-fieldwork design, as social surveys and experiments generally do, the strategy and even direction of the research can be changed relatively easily, in line with changing assessments of what is required by the process of theory construction. (Hammersley and Atkinson, 1983, p. 24)

Thus methods must be also be flexible and dynamic to accommodate these processes of 'funnelling' (Dey, 1993) and 'progressive focus' (Hammersley and Atkinson, 1983) which may easily change direction: static methods of analysis are not faithful to the spirit of ethnography. Furthermore, the extent to which methods of analysis are static or dynamic affects (or at least reflects) the analyst's relation to his/her data. For a dynamic approach to analysis involves shifts in interpretation, a continual sharpening and redefinition of old categories alongside the introduction of new ones, and all these processes necessitate strategies of rereading and reanalyzing the data.

The extent to which coding is a dynamic and flexible process depends largely on the type of coding scheme adopted, and the way it is applied to data; in short, it depends upon the attitude and skills of the researcher, and the readiness to go back and make changes to already coded data, which can be difficult and extremely time consuming. For those researchers who take on board the importance of flexible coding, it requires quite a skill to be constantly concerned about the implications of newly developed categories for previously coded data, and minimizing the possibility of forgetting to make the necessary modifications.

However, it is suspected that this dynamic potential of the coding strategy, albeit difficult to achieve, is limited to the stage of manual coding and analysis: once the data have been coded and entered into ETHNOGRAPH, and the 'real' exploratory analysis begins, the representation of data in terms of codes will become static and frozen to a large extent. Thus it is as soon as software intervenes in analysis that the characterization of data becomes rigid.

Entering codes into ETHNOGRAPH

When should data entry take place?

The apparent simplicity of this question is deceiving, since the stage at which codes are entered into the software has important technical implications for the coding of data. Originally, we decided not to enter the codes into 'ETHNOGRAPH' until the data had been completely coded by hand, rather than doing it as individual sections were completed. This would enable us more readily to meet the needs of the cumulative and dynamic nature of ethnographic analysis, allowing older categories to be changed and become sharper during the coding process. For we suspected that updating codes and boundaries would be much easier if still in the manual stage. In other words, we had little faith in ETHNOGRAPH's ability to cope with the unpredictable nature of qualitative analysis in this respect: its representation of coded data would largely be fixed and static, and thus the later this occurred the better.

Thus coding the data proceeded in two distinctive and successive stages: manual coding of all data followed by entering codes into the program. This enabled researchers, between stages, to go through the data as a whole and make the inevitable adjustments to codes and boundaries before they were entered into the computer. (Indeed, in retrospect it seems that this decision was a sensible one since, despite the program's numerous functions to correct codes and boundaries, it is technically an impossible task to make all changes that were made manually.) Furthermore, this strategy provided an additional opportunity to update codes as they were entered into the software. For, by organizing the data preparation process into two distinct stages, fieldnotes may be examined and codes checked three times before they become stored in the computer (figure 2.5).

For example, let us return to the category 'training'. As more data were coded with this category, the category acquired a more clearly defined meaning. In particular, it became distinguished from another category, education. When this became apparent, data which had been coded with either of these codes had to be checked. Furthermore, as we accumulated more understanding of the different ways in which ideas about training are manifest in data, we decided to replace the general code (training), with two more specific codes (training+, training-) which would represent these various manifestations more precisely. As soon as this decision was taken, previously coded data (the first few days of fieldnotes) had to be recoded with these new codes. The recoding, onset by both developments, is by no means unproblematic. However, making changes would technically be much more difficult, and time consuming, if we had already entered codes into ETHNOGRAPH.

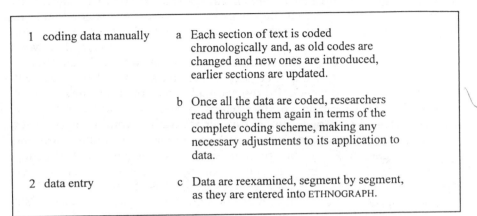

1 coding data manually	a Each section of text is coded chronologically and, as old codes are changed and new ones are introduced, earlier sections are updated.
	b Once all the data are coded, researchers read through them again in terms of the complete coding scheme, making any necessary adjustments to its application to data.
2 data entry	c Data are reexamined, segment by segment, as they are entered into ETHNOGRAPH.

Figure 2.5   Phases of coding data are organized around distinct stages of data preparation.

Once all the data had been coded, we were able to take a broader, more comprehensive look at the fieldnotes. The data were reread in terms of the complete list of categories, with particular emphasis on categories that had developed late in the coding process. For example, the categories 'competence' (the condition of being capable to execute duties) and 'skill' (a special ability) were later developed in addition to training. We can thus check that the distinctions between these categories are correctly reflected in the way data are coded. Methodological memoranda, showing the dates that categories are created, as well as the researchers' anticipations about their implications for previously coded data, are a valuable resource here. Again, any necessary changes are made before codes are entered into the program.

Finally, coded data can be rechecked at a microscopic level, where attention is drawn to each segment, as its assigned codes are entered into ETHNOGRAPH. Here we were able to check that a segment had been coded with all relevant codes. But, by and large, only the occasional, minor change was required in this phase of data preparation.

Since researchers are given these opportunities to adapt their characterization of the data, they should be fairly satisfied with their coding scheme and its application to the text, before it takes on a more fixed and inflexible form. Thus, in sum, this method of structuring the coding process seems to be the most sensible way of accommodating the unpredictable and inductive nature of ethnographic analysis within the coding strategy.

Faithful coding?

Despite the principles underlying this strategy, it is possible that its advantages may be translated into disadvantages in terms of validity. In particular, it became questionable whether it was necessarily a good thing to be able to change the original characterization of coded data so readily. For we began to realize that, as codes were entered into the software, data were only reexamined if codes were questioned, and codes were only questioned if they appeared in an unexpected way; if the codes attached to a segment did not seem to correspond to any particular pattern, then they will be rechecked against the data. In other words, it seems that while coding the data researchers construct (not always consciously) working hypotheses about the relations between categories. Also, it seems that implicit working hypotheses determine whether prior interpretations of the text are readily accepted or questioned and changed. Thus, these assumptions and untested hypotheses affect the way researchers look at and classify the data.

If one implication of this is that changes are made to bring 'deviant' data in line with inarticulated hypotheses, this is likely to undermine the validity of our interpretations; while trying to make sense of data and construct evidence, a superficial structure may be imposed on, and thereby distort, the reality under study. This is especially important considering the epistemological stance of ethnography. A similar observation is made by Shipman (1981, p. 145):

> It is inconsistent to support a method that denies the validity of imposing pre-determined structure on those observed, but to impose a structure on their accounts. There has to be an account of accounts, but the reality of the actor has to be respected from start to finish.

The process of coding data renders it difficult to respect the 'reality of the actor' from start to finish, as the assignment of codes depends upon the sensitivity of researchers to patterns in variables or categories in general, rather than patterns in data at hand.

Thus, while this coding strategy encourages the rereading of the text and familiarization with both data and analytical categories, ideas about patterns and relations are at the same time developing as researchers try to make sense of the data. Researchers need to be aware of these preliminary hypotheses (indeed they should explicitly explore them in analytic memoranda), and the possible ways that these may be directing the coding process in ways that do not represent the content of data. Otherwise, since data retrieval is based on the way data are coded (and theory-building, in turn, is based on comparing and contrasting recontextualized data, constructing hypotheses, and searching for confirming and disconfirming evidence), unrepresentative coding which is not faithful to the reality under study, is a very serious methodological problem.

This seems to be a general difficulty with the coding strategy, which encourages us to grow utterly dependent on our categories and the way they classify data. But it is also an important consideration when deciding how to organize the process of data preparation. Certainly, it is clear that the decision regarding when to enter codes into software is not only a technical one of ensuring that codes can be changed when necessary: it also has methodological repercussions. But then again, if we were aware of the above dangers at the outset of our research, perhaps we could use each phase to check against unfaithful coding, rather than to check the cooccurrence of codes in terms of our developing ideas about the relations between categories.

Data retrieval and analysis

Searching for general topics and themes

In an earlier section, we examined some of the problems facing researchers when coding for both specific aspects of categories, and categories in general. In our research, we decided not to use codes to depict categories in their most general form, because this raised too many technical problems in meeting ETHNOGRAPH's code limit. Instead, codes which depicted a specific dimension or aspect of a topic or theme were assigned to segments, on the understanding that the distinctions between aspects of the same category could be collapsed, if we wanted to move to a higher level of generality or abstraction. In principle, generalizing searches may be attained in several ways, but unfortunately ETHNOGRAPH does not provide adequate support for any of them: it has no 'wildcard' facility, and its 'quasi-Boolean' facility (which enables researchers to specify the proximity of one code in relation to another to narrow a search) is too restrictive.

The conceptual position of a code in our coding scheme is denoted by the first few characters in its codeword. Where topics and themes are internally differentiated into smaller categories, they are still explicitly attached to these 'parent' categories because their names all share the same prefix. At the time, it seemed common sense to organize the coding scheme in this way; in retrospect, it seems that a deeper assumption was at work. This assumption was that, in the stage of data retrieval, we would be able to conduct a search on a general category simply by searching for all occurrences of this prefix, replacing the suffix with a wildcard character. Thus, by conducting a search on PRIV/?, we would be able to retrieve data relevant to all aspects of the theme 'privacy': first, the right of patients to shut out incoming information or be left in peace (PRIV/IN); second, the right for patients to control outgoing information, and the terms under which 'their business' is communicated to others (PRIV/OUT); and third, the patients' right to organize space and time according to their individual needs (PRIV/ORG). Similarly, we may generalize searches for topic codes, retrieving segments that had only been coded for a particular aspect of the topic, by dropping the suffixes '+' and '-' from the search code. Thus, all data relevant to the topic 'education' may be retrieved, irrespective of whether they had been coded with the code for expert knowledge and medical pedagogy (EDUCATION+), on the one hand, or lay knowledge and superstitious models of disease (EDUCATION-), on the other. However, ETHNOGRAPH does not permit the use of 'wildcards', or searches for truncated codes.

The other way in which it is possible to generalize searches, or to make them more inclusive, is to combine specified codes in a Boolean logic. If we wanted to find all data relevant to a category in general (such as the degree of fear or apprehension caused by impending danger or pain) we can link each specific code (FEAR+, FEAR-) with the 'or' operator (FEAR+ OR FEAR-). Data tagged with either code will then be retrieved. This is a more clumsy way of generalizing searches, because researchers have to specify each code to be included, which is quite time consuming if a category has many aspects or dimensions (for example, we had eight dimension codes for the theme 'social relations'). However, ETHNOGRAPH does not support the 'or' Boolean operator either. Rather, searches can only be made for a code that appears either with other specified codes (using the 'and' operator), or without other specified codes (using the 'not' operator). Yet these are both ways of making searches more exclusive; there is no obvious way of expanding searches to make them more general or inclusive.

The nearest approximation we can achieve with ETHNOGRAPH to an inclusive search, is to conduct a single search on each of the codes. For example, to search for all data relevant to 'flexibility' in general, one search would be made for 'FLEX+' and one for 'FLEX-'. We can specify all required codes at the outset of a search (this gives the impression that only one search is being made) but the program still takes a long time to complete the process (it searches through a whole file for one code, before beginning to search for the next code in the same file). But, as figure 2.6 illustrates, the data retrieved by two single searches is not the same as if we were able to search for 'FLEX+ or FLEX-' (or, equally, 'FLEX?'). In short, those segments assigned with both categories will be retrieved in both searches, resulting in unnecessary duplication of data. Thus data recontextualized in terms of general categories will not be organized in a way which is immediately amenable to analysis.

Indeed, we found ETHNOGRAPH's search facility disappointing all round. This may be because it did not fit our organizing system very well, or we had unfounded expectations about the versatility of code-and-retrieve software. In any case, our experience certainly illustrates that the nature of a program's search facility needs to be fully considered before the coding scheme is developed. For the types of searches available affect the efficiency of codes as tools of retrieval. More generally, this draws attention to a problem which is commonly experienced by new users of any software: it is

56

not sufficient to learn about software limitations as they come to light, because this could easily result in the need to adapt whole sets of codes, or even abandon the coding scheme altogether. However, equally, it is impossible to prevent such problems from arising by examining all the technical literature about software at the outset of a project. This is because manual information bears little meaning for the user until the stage that is being described has been reached in practice.

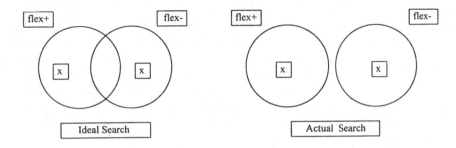

Figure 2.6   Contrasting text retrieved with different types of searches for the general category 'flexibility'. The Venn diagram on the left represents a search using the 'or' operator, whereas the one on the right represents two individual searches on codes. In both diagrams, 'x' marks the data that are retrieved.

Quantitative aspects of data

Analyzing the quantitative aspects of data may be an important way of generating meaning, or provide one way of 'getting to know the data', in early stages of qualitative analysis. Also, the distribution of codes over a given data file, or the data as a whole, may give us an initial focus or research question which is necessary to get the analysis going. For example, researchers may want to begin their analysis by asking questions about the code that is used most often to tag data in a given file. In addition, distributions may be of methodological interest, because they draw attention to codes that dominate certain sections of the data, and this can trigger the asking of methodological questions.

For example, it occurred to us that the fact that a code dominates a particular section of the fieldnotes does not necessarily imply that these topics or variables are the most significant in those data. Rather, uneven distribution may be an artefact of the researcher's relationship to the data, reflecting the fluctuations and changes in focus characteristic of this relationship. Seen in these terms, concentrations of codes may be due to at least three extraneous factors. First, the data collector (in this case, Roth) may have had certain issues in mind during a day's fieldwork so that things relating to such issues were noticed more readily than those relating to others. Second, the ethnographer may have had certain issues in mind when reflecting on a day's fieldwork, so that the corresponding fieldnotes were dominated by such issues; whether awareness of them came before, during, after the fieldwork itself. Third, certain issues may have been prominent in the minds of analysts (us) while coding the data, so that coded data reflects the special attention given to these issues.

In other words, by the time data are coded, the same reality has been interpreted, constructed and reconstructed three consecutive times. Special attention given to any issues at any point in this process will be reflected in its outcome: there will be an uneven distribution of codes throughout the data. This is an important methodological point because what happens during these processes of interpretation and construction are vital for the following stage - the main stage of data analysis. Indeed, if data collection and analysis runs in a linear process (like ours did out of necessity), each stage is shaped by the stage that comes before it, and has implications for the one that follows it. This is especially the case when a coding strategy is adopted, because analysis can only build upon that which has already been given a foundation in the previous stage. Any ideas emergent from the present stage of data retrieval, which have not been anticipated to some extent in the coding stage, cannot usually be incorporated into the main analysis without effectively starting the process over again, and this is likely to be highly time consuming and problematic.

However, despite these reasons for looking at the quantitative aspects of data, ETHNOGRAPH's facilities for examining the distributions of codes again fall short. Although it provides 'code frequency lists', it only does so for individual files rather than across files for the data as a whole. Thus, we are unable to get a holistic feel for code distributions, and this may have provided a useful way to transcend the misleading impact of codes dominating particular sections, as outlined above. In particular, it would be useful if the program could draw a graph or table, displaying the distribution of codes for a specified range of data. These facilities may be improved, however, with the next version of ETHNOGRAPH, which will be able to make some statistical tabulations both within and between files (Seidel et al., 1988).

Of course the frequency of codes is only one aspect of their distribution in the data. A code's frequency only indicates how often it is applied to the text: it says nothing about how much of the text is actually tagged with it. This second aspect of distribution - the amount of data tagged with a particular code - is also important if researchers want to examine the quantitative dominance of a particular code. But again, ETHNOGRAPH does not help us calculate this very easily. It seems that the only way to do this is to conduct a single search on one code and then manually compare the length of data output to that of other code searches.

It may also be useful to examine the distribution of codes at a more specific, detailed level. Here, we may ask questions such as 'are segments tagged with a particular code always engulfed by larger segments belonging to other codes?' Or, conversely, 'do segments tagged with a particular code consistently contain smaller segments belonging to another code and, if so, in what other contexts do these smaller codes occur?' Such questions are important because the distribution of codes in terms of where they figure in nests and overlaps is likely to have methodological, as well as analytical, implications. By asking these questions, a greater understanding of the relations between categories may develop. More importantly, they need to be considered to be aware of any effect that the distribution of codes may have on how data are interpreted at this stage of analysis. Otherwise the effect would remain implicit and this would compromise the maxim that research results should not be method-dependent (i.e. any conclusions drawn from Roth's fieldnotes using the coding segments strategy are specific to this strategy of analysis only). Thus, such considerations are important to all researchers.

Before some of these questions are applied to the Roth data, however, it is worth noting a general observation which emerged from reflection upon the above points. In retrospect, it seems that the very existence of ETHNOGRAPH's code frequency list facility is enough to initiate a whole process of thinking in which quantitative questions about data and codes are asked. At the outset of the search and retrieval stage of analysis, when researchers are looking for initial ways to penetrate and represent data, all such facilities which are quick to administer will be used. ETHNOGRAPH makes qualitative knowledge about codes for individual files easy. But this does not have much analytical significance in itself. Rather, it encourages the asking of other questions regarding, for example, quantitative aspects of data across files. ETHNOGRAPH cannot, however, accommodate such questions. Thus, to satisfy their curiosity, researchers will be engaged, before they know it, in the time-consuming activities of tabulating numbers and drawing graphs. Will the net effect of this be that much more time in qualitative studies will be concerned with the pursuit of quantitative questions? It certainly seems that the coding segments strategy, as represented by ETHNOGRAPH, encourages the kinds of 'analytic madness' identified by Seidel (1991), outlined in the first chapter of this book.

Analyzing patterns of codes for a typical theme

This section illustrates some of the issues hitherto raised in this chapter, by describing some of the initial decisions made at the beginning of the retrieval stage of analysis. More specifically, we will explore the first few questions about coded data encouraged by ETHNOGRAPH, triggered by its various facilities and the way it displays coded data. In particular, it is argued that nearly all decisions regarding the selection of a category to work with, and the questions that are asked about that category, relate to the quantitative aspects of coded data.

Choosing a category The first thing we wanted to do was select a typical theme to get started on, and open our analysis. In order to find a 'typical' theme, we considered various things about each category. First, we needed to get an idea of the distribution of categories. For this end, we instructed ETHNOGRAPH to create a code frequency list, which displays each code in order of the number of segments to which they are assigned. (The program also gives the option of displaying codes and their frequencies in alphabetical order, if preferred.) Second, we needed to consider the number of dimensions defining each category. By referring to our coding scheme list, we could see that these ranged from one to three for those categories which had only one level of subcategories, and between six and eight for those that had several levels of subcategories. Finally, we wanted to chose a theme that was of obvious importance given the choice of field.

In light of these considerations, we decided to focus the initial analysis on 'hygiene'. This category focuses on those ideas and practices concerned with cleaning the environment (HYG/ENV) or the human body (HYG/PER), to eradicate or minimize the presence of dust, germs, and other 'dirty' effects of disease. Hygiene is a typically thematic category in our coding scheme, in that it has two dimensions. It also has a mid-range frequency, and is evenly distributed throughout the fieldnotes as a whole. Finally, hygiene was chosen because how and why certain practices become constructed as hygienic or unhygienic is a central concern for anyone conducting an ethnographic study of a TB hospital. Thus, having selected our first category to work with, we conducted a single search on both of its dimensions (HYG/ENV and HYG/PER), and then began asking questions about it to focus our reading of the retrieved data. The first thing we were interested in was not so much the content of the retrieved data, but rather the other codes that were attached to the same data, as shown by ETHNOGRAPH's mode of display. Basically, we began looking for any pattern in the appearance of codes, such as where they figure in nests and overlaps.

The presence and absence of other codes It is possible to draw some meaning about the data simply from looking at the codes assigned to them. For example, figure 2.7 depicts a segment retrieved in a search on personal hygiene. Without reading the data of the segment, we know that it describes a deviant incident or opinion involving a particular attendant, Bailey. We also know that this incident involves breaking rules about wearing masks. Similarly, we can draw conclusions about the data from the absence of codes. Since there is no code suggesting that a view is being expressed, we can assume that it is an incident that is being reconstructed. We can also deduce that the analytic interest of this segment lies not in its capture of ideas about how the disease is transmitted from one thing to another, since it is not tagged with the code for contamination(CONTAM). Rather than being about whether wearing a mask really prevents contamination, this segment may be about how a shortage of mask supplies necessitates rule-breaking, for example. In any case, the point is that by thinking about both the absence and presence of codes, we can make assumptions about the analytical content of data, and this is an activity which is encouraged by ETHNOGRAPH's mode of display for retrieved segments.

```
search: hyg/per
```

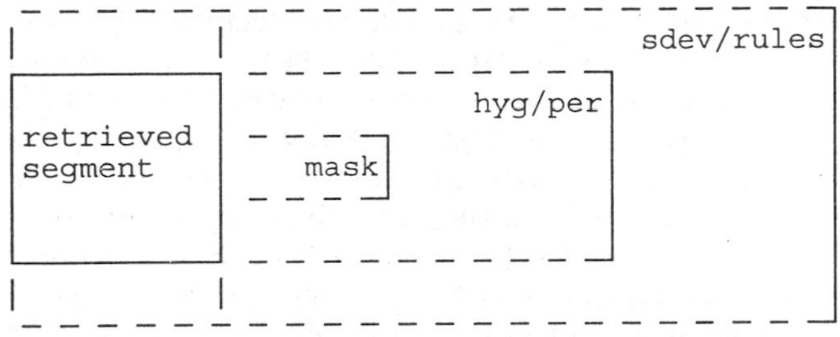

Figure 2.7 **Internal and external segments in a single search on personal hygiene. Whereas internal segments (MASK) are always completely retrieved in a search, external segments (SDEV/RULES) are always only partially visible: only the overlapping data are retrieved.**

Patterns in nests and overlaps Furthermore, it is not only the presence of a code that tells us something about a segment: its position in relation to other codes can also be significant as a meaning-building tool. For example, the positions of codes in figure 2.7 suggest that the event concerning the mask is but one form of deviance regarding hygiene rules (because the former is an internal segment of the latter), and the deviant act captured by the segment is recalled in a wider context of rule-breaking by this member of staff - it is not a one-off incident. Perhaps more importantly, the positions of codes in nests and overlaps can suggest relations between categories. This possibility directed our reading of the recontextualized data for the first time, when we asked 'do segments external and internal to those defined by HYG/PER consistently belong to certain codes?'

Focusing first on external segments, which are the outermost levels of nests and only partially in view in single searches, an examination of the recontextualized data did not yield anything new. There was only one anomaly, which concerned the distribution of the code for the topic 'contamination'. When designing the coding scheme, we anticipated that topics would be subsumed under themes. Yet it appeared nearly always in conjunction with both aspects of hygiene. This was not altogether surprising however. This is because we knew that this category had acquired new meaning during the coding process: contamination had become a more general category which rendered it more thematic than topical. For although it was originally devised as a topic depicting the meanings of disease transmission, it became clear while coding data that these meanings were often merged with more general social phenomena: cleansing ritual, moral pollution, and the expression of cultural difference (see Weaver, 1994). Thus the category came to include a wide range of ideas about how people were defined as clean, as well as how they become dirty and infected; and not only with regard to TB. Thus, contamination no longer depicted a specific set of ideas about hygiene, as did 'bugs', for example.

Similarly, most of the codes assigned to internal segments (I.E AIR, AUTOCLAVE, BEDMAKING, BUGS, CLEAN, CLOTHES, DIRT, FEAR+, FOOD, MASK) were in line with our expectations about the categories which tended to be specific to the theme of hygiene. Indeed most of these were expected to be exclusive to hygiene because it is in relation to this theme that such codes were developed. However, the search on HYG also threw up other codes which were not designed in relation to this theme. All of these categories were expected to be fairly independent, not being attached to any theme in particular (e.g. authority, conflict, diligence, gossip, identity, training, etc). None of those retrieved were unexpected in that they had been conceptualized only in relation to other themes.

Not only did the distribution of codes suggest nothing really new about the relation of hygiene to categories represented by topic codes: it also failed to say anything new about the relation of this theme to other themes. The distribution of thematic codes in relation to hygiene would be of value only to outsiders who had not experienced the process of coding, and its contingent accumulation of knowledge of the data.

Furthermore, the search on hygiene did not suggest anything new about the relation between themes and topics in general. However, this is partly because our expectations had changed during the process of coding data: they were not the same at the outset of our research when the coding scheme was first designed. At that stage, it was believed that there would be a clear distinction between the data (and codes) retrieved by thematic and topic/variable codes because of their perceived differences shown below:

- abstract/conceptual/general thematic codes
- concrete/empirical/specific topic codes

However, while applying the codes to the text, it became clear that the distinction was much more ambiguous and complex. Codes did not fit neatly into this scheme: some topics (e.g. contamination), were more abstract than empirical and were used more frequently and consistently throughout the data than were some thematic categories (e.g. sex divisions), and vice versa. This means that, during the retrieval and analysis stage, researchers cannot explicitly control the direction of their analytical path (i.e. whether moving from concrete to abstract or from abstract to concrete) in the straightforward way first imagined. This assumption is due to a flaw in thinking about categories as arranged in a linear continuum. A multidimensional approach to categories seems necessary, but this approach was not one encouraged by the coding strategy at the outset of analysis. (The fifth chapter in this book explains how this approach to categories contrasts with that encouraged by a hypertext strategy.)

Conclusion Since there is nothing much surprizing about the presence or absence of codes in this search, or about the arrangement of internal and external segments, and nothing new about the data seems to have been revealed, we are left wondering whether the process of decontextualization and recontextualization has been worthwhile. But although the examination of internal and external segments, and the distribution of codes more generally, proved not to be inspiring for new openings of analysis, there is one distinct advantage of looking at these distributions. While looking at the codes that had been thrown up in the search, the researchers realized that they could give reasons why each category was retrieved in the search, and hence give instances of how each category was related to hygiene without having read the retrieved data themselves. This points to the usefulness of codes as retrieval devices in human - as well as computer - memory.

In other words, looking at the way codes are organized in relation to recontextualized data did not provide anything new to add to analytical memos regarding the qualitative development of categories and concepts. But what the codes did provide was a set of prompts or key words which enabled researchers to retrieve relevant information from memory. If, from a single conjunction of codes, we are able to remember a string of appropriate data, this may prove to be an efficient way of keeping as much relevant information as possible at hand, and thereby be an important asset to data analysis and theorizing. Furthermore, this seems to suggest that the coding process does indeed facilitate a strong sense of familiarity with the data. But it must be realized that this familiarity is only in terms of the way they have been categorized: with codes. Of course, knowing the data only in terms of codes, as opposed to ways characteristic of other strategies, fundamentally affects the analysis process. (This will become clearer in later chapters as the other analytic strategies are examined.)

In sum, the questions examined in this section provoke the following general observation: although researchers may believe that the coding process is essentially a phase of data preparation, this is, in fact, where the value of the coding segments strategy lies. Technical problems associated with software limitations which constrain this process aside, developing an organizing system and coding the data are the most creative parts of analysis with ETHNOGRAPH. Paradoxically, what is considered to be the 'real' stage of analysis, the search and retrieval of data segments, is actually rather mechanical and does not uncover any new ground. The latter stage is more a process of 'tidying up' or concluding the coding process, than a stage of evoking and exploring new ideas.

After completing several searches and reading through the retrieved data, we found instances where data segments had not been coded for all those categories to which they were relevant. For example, the following text is concerned with the conceptualizations of space and the risk of contamination, yet it was not coded with the corresponding code ORG/SPACE:

> Bailey described how Walters would scrub her arms all the way up to the elbows after she's been out in the patient area even if she hasn't touched anything

If data relevant to this category are continually not coded as such, theoretical development of ideas about how space is related to contamination will be impeded: indeed this relation may even be overlooked altogether. This could be devastating if the connection between categories is a vital aspect of each topic or theme (as is the one in our example).

This may well have been because we forgot to consider some codes while coding. After all, the relevance of a piece of text to analytical categories is not always obvious: often it has to be thought about in relation to categories long and hard before such decisions are made. (Indeed, this is one of the demands which makes coding such a laborious process and yet also, on the other hand, one which encourages such a deep understanding of the data.) But even where the relevance of a piece of text to an analytical category is obvious, there were still occasions where those codes which should have been foremost in our minds (because of their obvious relevance) were not applied to the text during the coding process.

For example, take the following excerpt from the fieldnotes:

> Farrell and Bailey were both very angry for Holt for upsetting the patients in this way for what they considered no good reason at all. 'That's your educated attendant for you', said Nora.

This segment describes condemnation of the lack of professional integrity of a particular member of staff. It also implies that this lack of integrity is generalized to the occupation (attendant) of the accused figure (Holt). These are important aspects of the analytical category of 'identity', which we defined as 'the rights, duties, and moral responsibilities of staff, as defined by perceptions of occupational structure (both specifically in the hospital and generally in society).' Yet the significance of this category apparently was not recognized during the coding process: the code IDENTITY was not assigned to the segment.

Alternatively, such lapses during the coding process could be due to the fact that, without having gone through this process, researchers would not have perceived the relevance of segments of text to other categories in any case. In other words, it is only through the processes of decontextualization and recontextualization, and their entailing accumulation of knowledge, that this perception was made possible in the first place. This is an optimistic perspective which interprets what may otherwise be seen as a pitfall of the coding strategy, as proof that the strategy works: the process of decontextualization and recontextualization is worthwhile because the experience of each stage throws new light on the data and our analytical categories.

Either way, it may be concluded that knowledge of the data which is gained during the coding process, is actually more reliable than the end product of this process - the coded data - itself. Thus, the coding segments strategy may be seen as useful in that it facilitates a sensitive relationship between researchers and their data. However, this does not in itself answer the essential question 'to what extent does it facilitate data analysis?' If one is continually finding fault with prior interpretations of the data, as embodied in the coded text, how can the analysis based on these insufficient interpretations be expected to be successful?

Static or dynamic?

In short, analysis cannot be successful unless the data as a whole are reexamined and recoded. This interpretation, in turn, may also become inadequate and demand that data are, again, recoded in the future. Thus, qualitative analysis using this strategy consists of progressive layers of interpretations, with each new interpretation affecting the way researchers look at the old, and necessitating the latter's adaptation so that analysis may proceed. Thus, for ETHNOGRAPH to aid qualitative analysis, it must be flexible enough to make any necessary changes to the codes which were produced and applied during our first interpretation of the data.

Technically, the program allows the researcher to recode the data with relative ease. We are permitted to change or delete the line definitions of specific segments or codes in specific instances, or we can 'globally' change or delete codes for a set of files. But despite these facilities the process itself is complex. This is because the changes which are most likely to be necessary are fundamental: redefining the meaning of categories. By changing the meaning of one code we are likely to affect the meaning of others, since they are all related to and contingent upon each other, and thereby affect their relevance and application to the text. Thus, perhaps analysis with ETHNOGRAPH is not as flexible as it first would seem, although this is likely to be a methodological weakness of the coding segments strategy in general rather than of ETHNOGRAPH in particular.

Furthermore, it would seem that progressive research (according to the grounded theory tradition), requires movement not only between interpretations, but also back to the original data (in their original form and context, free of codes). For even if our interpretations had originally emerged from the data, without being continually recursive such constructions of reality may become distorted and artificial, or at the very least vague. Thus it is often necessary to view the data in their original form and context, rather than in terms of codes, as a methodological check. This may counteract, for example, some of the methodological problems of unfaithful coding, as discussed earlier in this chapter. But to what extent does ETHNOGRAPH enable this movement?

Technically, the retrieval of the original text is not a problem. We may view the original data on the computer monitor in its 'numbered' (as opposed to its 'coded') form at any time, or even efficiently find a particular section of text by specifying its location in terms of its filename and line numbers. However, what we cannot do using this program, is scroll or browse through the text outside, or even go backwards within, that which has been specified. The ability to browse text outside limits set by programs is an integral part of analysis. Thus at times it may be easier to analyze the hard copy of the original text rather than relying on ETHNOGRAPH.

In this respect, the program's representation of the text is rather static: data are rigidly divided into segments, and researchers must specify the text to be found in terms of the line numbers which constitute the segment. This implies prior knowledge of the segment, however, since the location of the phenomena of interest will already need to be specified. At the other extreme, if the precise location is unknown, researchers must indiscriminately scroll through the whole text. Here we have another aspect of Blank's (1989, p. 10) 'Goldilock's problem' of too much structure, on the one hand, and not enough, on the other. This problem is accentuated with code-and-retrieve software if they are unable to collate data on the basis of a certain characteristic of the text (a word or a combination of words). With ETHNOGRAPH, data can only be collated on the basis of a characteristic of an interpretation of the text (a code or a combination of codes).

Codes are not inherent to the data; rather, they are inherent to the interpretation of the data. They are products of a particular attempt to reconstruct the reality from which the data are extracted sociologically and textually. Seidel (1991, p. 114) warns of this problematic aspect of coding:

> we must be very careful about how we treat the coding process and what we do with the 'coded' data during the analytic phase. My perspective is that the things we identified in our data are artefacts of a relation we have with our data. The danger is that we will start taking these for granted. We will reify these things as objects and then base our understandings of the phenomena on these reified objects and, in the process, lose the phenomena.

This may prove to be one respect in which lexical searching programs are superior. With FYI, searches on the text in its original form may be completed by specifying a characteristic of the text, and without placing superficial constraints on the retrieval of data, since researchers may scroll through the document if they so desire. Perhaps this weakness of ETHNOGRAPH may be overcome if it is used in conjunction with FYI, relying on the latter whenever it is necessary to examine the original text.

During coding, we were continually concerned that decisions regarding the definition of segments would affect analysis in the search and retrieval stage of research. As we have now conducted sample searches on codes, and analyzed recontextualized· data, we are in a position to think again about some of the questions raised earlier. For example, how do decisions made during coding about segment boundaries, affect the quality of data retrieval? Is there too much or too little contextual information included in retrieved segments, and what effect does this have on data analysis?

For those segments defined by thematic codes, boundaries seemed useful and appropriate, in that enough contextual information was included in the segment to understand the phenomenon of interest. It is suspected that this is because of the 'umbrella' nature of these codes, which disposes them to be attached to whole sections of text (usually paragraphs), and to concur with the original structure of the text. This, to some extent, is likely to reduce the risk of contextual and boundary problems. If this is true, then the situation is more complex for topic codes. Since topics are more specific and exclusive categories, and they are attached to smaller segments which are subsumed under segments defined by thematic codes, more contextual problems will be experienced with topic codes. This will now be illustrated with an example.

'Education' is a topic which focuses on how ideas about disease fit into the dominant (scientific) model of disease. For example, if the data segment at hand captures a general conversation in which TB contamination is explained with reference to 'bugs crawling on the floor', the code EDUCATION- is applied, denoting that this view is characteristic of lay models of TB and superstitious attitudes to disease. Thus, EDUCATION- may sometimes represent, in data, a specific aspect of the more general topic of contamination: the model implicated in ideas about how people and things become contaminated with TB. Contamination, in turn, may be seen as one aspect of the category 'hygiene', which is concerned with the preservation of cleanliness, and the repression of dirt. These kinds of relationships between categories encourage nested or overlapping coding. For example, there are a lot of situations where segments coded with EDUCATION- are contained within larger segments coded with CONTAM and, larger still, HYG/PER or HYG/ENV. In such cases, the analyst will encounter contextual problems with smaller segments, regarding their relation to external nested layers, in single searches.

For instance, figure 2.8 displays a segment that was retrieved in a single search on EDUCATION. Although this segment encapsulates Roth's observation of the lack of conformity to medical models of TB contamination implied in nursing procedures, we do not know how he reached this conclusion; there are no details about what led him to make this comment included in the segment. ETHNOGRAPH's mode of display helps us to some extent here, for it indicates which codes are attached to external segments: CONTAM and HYG/PER (ep/contam identifies the stretch of action, to which this segment belongs, as an analytically significant episode). However, since the external segments themselves are not retrieved, the respect in which education is related to contamination and hygiene is lost. If we were able to see the whole nest, we would also see the codes belonging to other segments internal to personal hygiene, appear slightly earlier in the fieldnotes. If we knew that 'BUGS', 'AIR', 'BEDMAKING', 'HANDS', 'FOOD', 'ORG/SPACE', 'CLOTHES', AND 'MASK' were also part of the same nest as education, then this would help us think about the ways in which education is related to contamination and hygiene in this instance. This would give us the opportunity to read contextual data, which is important in itself. These practices of reading the context of a targeted segment, both in terms of attached codes and the data themselves, are clearly necessary for the development of theoretical categories. But they are not supported by ETHNOGRAPH.

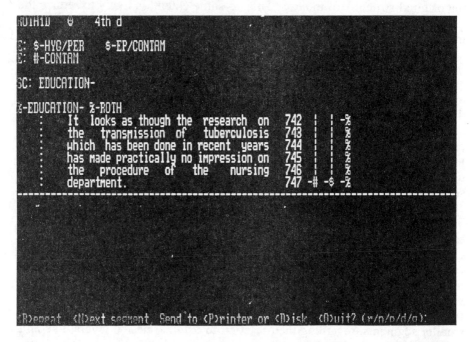

Figure 2.8 **An ETHNOGRAPH screen, showing a segment retrieved in a single search on the code EDUCATION-. The display mode indicates the other codes belonging to the segment, including those of external segments (larger levels of nests and overlaps).**

If researchers move in the same direction as in our research (first, completing single searches on all topics; second, looking at the retrieved data and recognizing certain relations within them; and third, developing hypotheses about these relations via the conduction of multiple searches on the relevant codes), these connections may be overlooked altogether because of the unacknowledged presence of contextual problems in earlier single searches. And this problem is not limited only to single searches: even with multiple searches, where the analyst has the option of looking at internal or overlapping segments (or taking a 'big view' in ETHNOGRAPH's terminology), this problem is still evident. This is because we can only take a 'big view' of nests and overlaps if their codes are specified in the search. Thus, if we searched data for 'EDUCATION+ and CONTAM', we can see all the data relevant to these codes (rather than just their intersection), but we cannot then opt to see all of the outermost level of the nest: hygiene. Thus researchers must always be aware of these potential hazards when analyzing nested segments: it is necessary to look beyond the data retrieved in one particular search to discover the data content of external segments. But this questions the analytic usefulness of ETHNOGRAPH's searches, as facilities for efficient data retrieval and tools for qualitative analysis.

Moving from single to multiple searching

It would seem that there is a 'normal' path of analysis using ETHNOGRAPH which involves, as noted above, moving from 'single searching' to 'multiple searching'. For, as Tesch notes, after data are coded, they are still not ready for interpretation:

> From its 'natural' context In the data document, the segment is transferred to the 'conceptual' context of the analysis document. This document holds all 'instances' in the data that conceptually belong together, and nothing else. It represents one 'category'. Such a document enables researchers to see their data in this new conceptual light, and to make sense of them in that process of pattern discovery and interpretation we usually call qualitative analysis. (Tesch, 1989, p. 147)

With ETHNOGRAPH, it is only through 'single searches' that real exploratory analysis can begin. Reading the data in this new context provokes new ideas about them. Such new ideas may necessitate the definition of, and coding for, new categories. Nevertheless, ideas which arise as a result of single searches then need to be explored in greater detail. This is achieved by conducting multiple searches on combinations of codes. Also, it is through multiple searching that the connections between categories may be explored.

In practice, however, analysis in our research did not take this character: movement through the stages of coding and searching was determined by something else. While reading the results of a single search, we became aware that we approached the text with certain questions in mind, that had developed during the coding process. Rather than analyzing the material with an 'open mind', we selectively read the text in order to develop ideas about a particular phenomenon further, or the relations between social variables, which had emerged from our initial characterization of the text. For example, while reading through data retrieved in the search on hygiene, our attention was predominantly focused on the way particular ideas about contamination related to particular positions in the occupational division of labour, and how the views of some were enforced upon others. These questions, which were emergent from interaction with data during the coding process, directed our reading of recontextualized data. And this reading, in turn, directed the way data were recontextualized yet again via multiple searches.

If researchers subconsciously develop hypotheses about phenomena while coding, and these affect the way recontextualized data are analyzed, what implications does this have for the rest of analysis? If the function of single searches is to classify events in a sociologically meaningful way, in order to illuminate aspects of phenomena that had not previously been noticed in their original context, analysis may become focused, deductive and rigid too soon. Rather than 'opening up the enquiry', analytical activity may become concerned with developing, confirming and disconfirming hypotheses. Arguably, these activities should occur later - during multiple searches - where relations between variables can be examined in more detail.

In short, if underdeveloped hypotheses direct our reading of the data in early stages of analysis, this may lead to the premature closure of analytic avenues. For example, if we want to develop only our pre-existing ideas, what about all those potential ideas which may have emerged if recontextualized data had been read differently? What about the more obscure relations between categories that had not been observed in data during their original context? It seems that, to a large extent, the diversity of findings in exploratory research will be superficially restricted when this analytical approach is adopted.

Furthermore, the limitations of this approach to recontextualized data are compounded when we consider that all this time researchers are constantly looking at the data only in terms of their categories. While we are looking to develop our hypotheses in terms of already established categories, the development of new ones which have a better 'fit' with data will be impaired. Generally, categories were not questioned once the data were coded, and neither were they recognized as preliminary units of analysis, inevitably needing to be sharpened as knowledge accumulates. Rather, categories were taken to be static, permanent 'things'. Indeed, they were treated, as Seidel (1991) feared, as 'objects' in the data, rather than artefacts of a peculiar relation which, by its very definition, is dynamic and changing. This fact questions the accuracy of findings based upon such codes and the adequacy of this strategy to fulfil the requirements of the grounded theory approach to qualitative analysis. Thus, despite ETHNOGRAPH's capacity to accommodate the supposed flexibility of qualitative analysis (by allowing the researcher to change, delete and add codes to the data at any point during the research), the research process is unlikely to demand these facilities. With the coding strategy, 'funnelling' (Dey, 1993) or 'progressive focusing'

(Hammersley and Atkinson, 1983) requires the relation between coding, searching and analyzing, to become less dialectical and inductive, and more linear and deductive.

Narrative or technical culture?

The most fundamental reason why qualitative researchers are cautious about using computer software for analysis is expressed by Drass (1989, p. 156):

> It is important for qualitative researchers to realize that embedded in all text-processing software is a set of analytic procedures. These procedures reflect the assumptions made by programmers (and incorporated into a program's algorithms) about the 'typical' features and requirements of user applications; i.e., who will use the software, what type of text they will analyze, and how they will want to manipulate the text.

Many qualitative researchers are concerned that embedded in software are particular epistemological assumptions which are antipathetic to their interests. One aspect of this has been noted with regard to commercial database software:

> The most significant restriction on commercial software is the assumption that records are static entities into which text can be entered and later retrieved. Treating records as static entities fits well with a variable-oriented, technical culture approach to the text. It is less appropriate for the case-oriented approach preferred by many qualitative researchers. (Blank, 1989, p. 9)

Here, the answer seems to lie in the need for qualitative researchers to be involved in the design of specialist software. However, our methodological analysis of ETHNOGRAPH suggests that, perhaps even specialist software reflects a 'technical reading culture' which introduces new forms of knowledge, and new relations between the data and the researcher, into qualitative analysis. Thus, has the adoption of software had the effect of making the technical, problem-solving culture, from within which computer technology was originally developed, affect the analytical processes in qualitative research? In order to answer this question, we will first look at the coding process, which is a particular type of data reduction, or strategy of data organization.

An important preliminary to any type of analysis is data reduction or organization. Ragin and Becker (1989) look at the strategies of data reduction which dominate social research. Quantitative analysis is largely concerned with explaining variation across cases and is therefore characterized by variable-oriented strategies. With this approach,

> We look at isolated facts about people (e.g., their different income levels) or other observational units and relate them to other isolated facts (e.g., their educational levels) in the aggregate. This type of data

reduction requires selective attention to limited aspects of the things we study. Cases are disaggregated into variables and distributions before any analysis takes place (1989, p. 49).

Despite working in the guise of qualitative analysis (which, according to Ragin and Becker, is case-oriented and concerned with comprehending diversity and creating 'holistic, integrative accounts of interrelated phenomena'), it seems that the approach to data reduction encouraged by the coding segments strategy is remarkably like that traditionally characteristic of quantitative research.

Although not concerned with the formal goals of the latter, the creation and manipulation of codes has similarities with the quantitative analyst's treatment of variables, as described by Ragin and Becker above. Via coding, data reduction involves the organization of data into topics. These categories may be seen, like variables, to represent limited aspects of the things we study and direct our attention toward these limited aspects. Furthermore, as argued earlier in this chapter, categories are treated as static permanent entities, and are thus attributed with the rigidity of variables, rather than artefacts of the researchers' developing conceptualization of data.

In addition to the coding process, which facilitates data to be disaggregated into variables, similarities with conventional quantitative analysis are continued in the search and retrieval stage with ETHNOGRAPH. Although not concerned with distributions to the same extent, ETHNOGRAPH encourages researchers to attribute some importance to code distributions. Once data have been coded, the distributions of codes in the data are given much attention (by examining ETHNOGRAPH's code frequency list, and by looking at the position of codes in nests and overlaps in recontextualized data. Thus, consideration of code distributions is something which continues throughout analysis: it is this practice which is believed to suggest theoretical relations between categories, and is the basis for decisions regarding which categories to pursue in more depth via search processes. Second, the code and retrieval stage of analysis has similarities with the 'technical culture' of quantitative research. As noted earlier in this chapter, coding software encourages the researcher to take the role of problem solver when reading the text, exploring and testing hypotheses about the relations between codes or variables. But the way this is achieved in the coding strategy does not respect the narrative of fieldnotes: rather, problems are constructed and explored only in relation to our coding or indexing of the data.

More generally, the coding strategy inscribed in software affects the structure of the research process, making it more similar to that of quantitative research. According to Ragin and Becker (1989), the research process comprises three different research activities (conceptualization, data collection, and data analysis) which relate differently to variable-oriented, quantitative research, on the one hand, and case-oriented, qualitative research, on the other. In the former, these three activities tend to be sharply differentiated and move in a linear direction, whereas in the latter there is a constant interaction and dialectical relation between these activities. However, Ragin and Becker also note that, the introduction of the microcomputer as an instrument of data reduction necessitates a degree of separation between these activities. They note, for example, that the 'simple task of structuring the input of the data requires a minimal level of prior conceptualization' (1989, p. 54). It is possible that such requirements make the qualitative research process less dialectical, less inductive, more structured, more linear, more rigid and, thereby, more similar to that of quantitative research.

Thus, in sum, the findings of our research may be taken as additional evidence for Ragin and Becker's claim:

> The available technical means of data reduction also have an impact on data reduction strategies, just as technical means affect all types of work. Thus, changes in these technical bases may affect both the changing character of sociological analysis and the gulf between different strategies of data reduction. (1989, p. 50)

ETHNOGRAPH to some extent encourages the qualitative researcher to approach the data as problem solver, and to use strategies of data reduction and analysis that are more characteristic of quantitative research.

The coding scheme in retrospect

While working with the coding segments strategy, it became apparent that an adequate analysis depended almost entirely on how the data were structured during the phase of data preparation or, more specifically, the adequacy of a system of codes and their application to the data. This demands the researcher to be very conscientious when developing an organizing system, which involves having to project forward continually to the phase of data analysis. For an adequate system of codes, researchers must be aware of the research questions they will want to explore in the main phase of analysis (via searches with ETHNOGRAPH), and this, in turn, requires a high degree of familiarity with the data. And yet how can this be achieved at such an early stage of the analysis? This paradox proved to be problematic for the coding strategy and, although there are several ways in which it could be resolved, the resolution can only ever be partial.

The first option is not to think at all about research questions at this stage and rather just develop a code when something in the data appears significant. This will have the methodological advantage of categories being emergent from the data alone, their development being uncontaminated by the interests and expectations of the researcher. Indeed, this seems to be the assumption at the heart of the coding strategy, and why it is believed that this method is so suited to ethnographic research. However, it can be argued that our secondary analysis of Roth's data was not due to any particular analytical question (only a methodological one) and yet the principle of developing categories as issues came to light seemed inappropriate (as discussed earlier in this chapter).

The other alternative is to develop a coding scheme that is so open and complex that a code may be developed for every aspect of an action or situation, whether or not they seem significant or relevant to a particular issue or topic. It was this method of developing an organizing system that was adopted in our project. Because this approach penetrated so many aspects of the data, it was able to accommodate enough flexibility and spontaneity in later analysis without having to predict its exact requirements, which would demand intricate knowledge of the data. However, this approach also brings new problems of its own. These problems will now be discussed with reference to the particular organizing system developed in our research. To recap, this consisted of four dimensions within which any act, idea, strategy, condition, or material object could be encompassed: general thematic codes; codes for specific topics; cast codes; and episodic codes.

The first problem was encountered when applying codes to data during the coding process. Because it was such an all-encompassing system of codes, we found that many segments required a large number of codes, often exceeding ETHNOGRAPH's limit. More specifically, a single segment was usually found to be relevant to several cast codes, topic codes, and thematic codes. This meant that predicaments such as those represented by figures 2.2 and 2.3 (p. 40) and their attached consequences, were far from uncommon.

Problems were also encountered during the main phase of analysis, which succeeded the coding process. It seems that data recontextualization achieved nothing that resembled 'data reduction'. Rather, searches generated a considerable mass of recontextualized data (far exceeding the quantity of original fieldnotes), much of which, as will be shown, remained just that. This mass of information can be overwhelming and stifling and, having reached this stage, researchers may therefore find it difficult to know what to do next. This is made especially difficult because not all of the information is analytically useful, and it is difficult to siphon the useful from the useless. The main reason for this is that researchers feel compelled to conduct a single search on most of the codes - even those that are seemingly insignificant or uninteresting.

The net result is that, where as many as twelve codes are attached to a single segment, the same segment will appear in as many as twelve different searches, but only a few of these will initiate new insights. This is due to the nature of our coding scheme and the fact that it was all-encompassing rather than selective, or designed to pursue particular questions or topics of interest. Thus, although our system avoided the necessity of anticipating the analytical activity of the next stage, it brings with it the greater possibility of many codes, and their corresponding recontextualizations of data, being analytically worthless.

This problem brings into question the commensurability between our coding scheme and the underlying principle of recontextualization. Recontextualization is the principle at the heart of the coding segments strategy and implies the duplication of data. The duplication of a segment is believed to represent the point in the data at which two codes intersect. For example, where a segment is coded for the categories of 'fear' and 'contamination', it needs to be examined in relation to both of these categories (as well as others) in order to appreciate and explore the relation between the phenomena represented by the codes. But the duplication of data may also be unnecessary. For example, categories varied widely in terms of their generality and specificity, and they often tended to be hierarchically related, which meant that the total data retrieved by a search on one code was often entirely retrieved by the search of another code. This is most common where topics, such as the use of masks or ideas about bugs and germs, are conceptually engulfed by a larger topic, such as contamination, or theme, such as hygiene (figure 2.9). Thus it is important to assess the analytical worth of thematic codes: will a search on a general code retrieve more than that data already associated with its smaller or more specific constituent topics? Will it have heuristic significance?

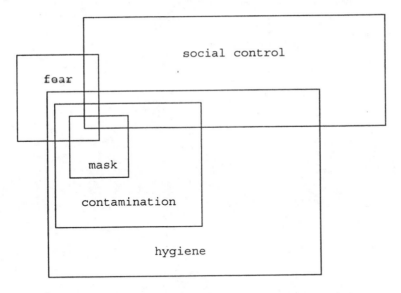

Figure 2.9 An example of ETHNOGRAPH's representation of categories, with intersections signifying a relation between categories (because they share data). These intersections are duplicated in the output of single searches, retrieved by themselves in multiple 'and' searches, and remain the only portions of coded data not to be retrieved in 'not' searches.

All of these problems are exclusive to the coding strategy. With hypertext, for example, the conceptual relations between categories are represented in the very structure of the hypertext so that duplication is unnecessary. Microcomputing strategies which do not involve duplicating the data, may be better able to accommodate those categories that are very general. Perhaps one reason for this is that other ways of searching or exploring the data are less mechanical (unlike with ETHNOGRAPH where researchers feel compelled to conduct single searches for all codes, automatically). Thus, researchers are less likely to be faced with the daunting task of sorting through a mass of information (much of which is insignificant). Such issues, among others raised in this chapter, will now be examined in relation to the lexical searching strategy.

3 Lexical searching

Introduction

Instead of searching and retrieving coded segments, or text that has been categorized in any sort of way, lexical search programs find words or phrases in the text, according to 'strings' specified by researchers. Sometimes known as 'text retrievers' (Tesch, 1990), these programs do not search for meaningful segments of text, and neither do they organize text (or recontextualize data) in a meaningful way. This is why Tesch (1990, p. 185) distinguishes them as 'search programs' rather than programs for qualitative analysis, and why they are left out of other text books for qualitative analysis altogether (e.g. Dey, 1993). However, although not designed specifically for this purpose, lexical search programs seem to have clear advantages for qualitative analysis.

Generally, they enable researchers to explore their data directly, by searching for lexical items and analyzing the lexical content of fieldnotes, interview transcripts, and any other documents of interest. By prompting the program to produce a vocabulary list, we can examine the vocabularies displayed by respondents, and thereby gain insights to how people articulate phenomena, or through language make sense of their everyday lives. Similarly, we may find that a certain word dominates interviews with a certain person, or certain social encounters, which may be analytically significant. Also, these programs enable us to conduct searches not only on particular words, but also combinations of words. In these searches, researchers can specify conditions for text to be retrieved, regarding the proximity of one word to another, by using a variety of Boolean operators in a search string.

Lexical searching software can be utilized by the qualitative researcher for several analytical purposes. Tesch (1990, p. 182) notes one possibility:

> Even researchers who normally deal with interpretational analysis, in which they handle meaningful chunks of text rather than words, could find some of these programs' options helpful. For instance, a researcher

may notice that a certain concept is alluded to in his/her data. As a validity check s/he could create a list of synonyms and phrases that capture that concept, and explore whether, and how frequently, it was directly addressed by the participants in his/her research.

Thus lexical search programs are a useful means of checking the validity of analyses shaped by other strategies, such as the coding segments strategy in interpretive research, or in the triangulation of methods (Tesch, 1990, p. 195). As well as being methodologically valuable for keeping in check the coding strategy, this combined approach is also economically viable: many lexical search programs are inexpensive to implement, in terms of time and money (FYI, GOFER, GOLDEN RETRIEVER, TEXT COLLECTOR, and TEXT ANALYZER require little preparation or indexing). As such, lexical searching may provide a complementary strategy to coding segments for many qualitative researchers. One aim of this chapter is to explore this possibility, with specific reference to FYI and ETHNOGRAPH. But lexical searching is not necessarily confined only to complementing other strategies. In some types of analysis, search programs are a valuable resource in themselves. The most obvious tradition here is content analysis. Indeed, some lexical search programs have been developed specifically for this purpose (for example, WORDMATCH, KWIC TEXT INDEX, CONTENT ANALYSIS and TEXTPACK).

According to Krippendorff (1980), content analysis is a method of inquiry into the 'symbolic meaning' of messages. The task for the researcher is to make explicit the context relative to which data are analyzed, including all conditions - whether antecedent, coexistent or consequent. The meaning of data is established by making inferences to certain aspects of their context. Then it is necessary, firstly, to summarize the data and represent them in a systematic way which enhances comprehension; secondly, to discover patterns and relationships within data which had not been perceived by the 'naked eye' and to test relational hypotheses; and, thirdly, to relate data obtained by content analysis to data obtained by other methods or in other situations, to reveal further information or for validation.

The most common way of representing data in content analysis is in terms of their frequency. Data are often represented or interpreted so that researchers may, for example, compare the frequency of one category with the average of all categories, or note the changes in frequencies over time. A second way of representing data is in terms of the relations between variables via associations, correlations and cross-tabulations. These relations may be either within the results of a content analysis or between the results of a content analysis and data obtained independently.

A popular analytic activity in content analysis is to construct images and portrayals. Another is to conduct discriminant analysis where the researcher is concerned with everything that is said about something or, when comparing cases, what is unique about something. As stated by Krippendorff (1980, p. 12), many content analyses 'focus on a special entity, person, idea or event and attempt to find out how it is depicted or conceptualized, what its symbolic message is'. Other techniques include the clustering of interrelated concepts (which reflects the way clusters are formed in reality, i.e. via semantic rather than purely analytic similarities), contextual classification (which assumes that symbols have more in common the more alike the context in which they occur), and contingency analysis (which aims to infer the network of a source's associations from the pattern of co-occurrences of symbols in messages).

Thus, at the outset it seems that our sample lexical search program, FYI300PLUS, will be invaluable to many qualitative researchers since it can be fitted to a variety of analytical goals. For example it may be first used to collate all information about a given word or symbol (for example 'bug') so that researchers may answer questions about who uses it, the conditions in which it arises, to what it refers etc. Similarly, it can be usefully employed to gather all information about specific actors, including how they are represented in the words and actions of others, as well as their actual behaviour as observed by the researcher. In these ways searching for words is a useful analytical technique in the case of both interview and fieldnote data. Both of these tasks are much more complicated using the coding segments strategy as they involve extensive preparation (all words of interest must be coded), and the limitations of software, regarding the number of codes which can be attached to the text, render this preparation even more complex.

Another way in which FYI may prove to be a valuable tool is when the researcher wants to grasp a particular phenomenon, theme, or idea. If interested in violence, for example, researchers could analyze the vocabulary of a document, looking for words which may relate to this phenomenon (such as hostility, frustration, anger etc), and then conduct searches on these words to see if they throw any new light on the construction of violence in social situations. For these reasons, searching with FYI may provide researchers with a powerful means of grasping the way actors construct their reality, and understand social processes and events. This chapter examines the ways in which such types of understanding contrast with or complement the coding strategy.

Data preparation

Like many lexical search programs, FYI needs no data preparation, as such. Researchers are not required to structure the text in any specific way and no prior understanding of the text is necessary before the retrieval and analysis stage. All that researchers need to do is import the data as ASCII and set up a filing system. At this point, researchers have to specify two things. First, they need to decide which words (if any) are not to be treated as key words. This enables analytically insignificant words, such as 'and' 'the' 'in' 'of' 'as' 'a', to be omitted from the search, and thereby speed up the search process. Second, researchers need to decide how much of the text will define a 'hit', which refers to the amount of co-text retrieved with a key word. In our research, we used the default options (representing the most popular choices) in both cases: all words were treated as keywords, and the paragraph consituted the hit. Once a filing system has been created, researchers can immediately begin to search and analyze the text. This is in direct contrast with ETHNOGRAPH which requires extensive coding of the text, before the program can retrieve segments. This is an important difference and one which has methodological implications. Lexical searching enables researchers to be much more spontaneous in exploring the data and following up ideas, and little effort is wasted if those ideas lead to analytical 'blind alleys'. More generally, this difference regarding required data preparation suggests a more fundamental difference in their respective assumptions about the analysis process. With FYI,this process does not have to be linear or characterized by rigid sequential stages.

Data retrieval and analysis

Key Word in Context (KWIC)

The KWIC facility is the essential tool of lexical searching computer strategies. Designed for the purpose of examining the lexical context of selected words, KWIC enables the researcher to examine the context-dependent meanings of key words, and thereby grasp their diversity of meaning. The ability to examine context-dependent meanings also enables researchers to explore the conditions for variations in meanings. By comparing their contexts, they may examine whether different senses of a particular key word coincide with different authors, actors, situations or documents. Thus, say we are interested in the meanings attached to contamination in Roth's data. By searching for 'contaminat*' and analyzing the lexical context in which this root word appears, or directing our attention to the presence or absence of other keywords, we can gain insights into the construction of contamination in the TB hospital. In particular, we may find that not only does its meaning for social actors vary according to their position in a social network but, furthermore, that its meaning is not static for each person: it is contingent upon the copresence and positioning of other personnel.

Thus, analytical interest becomes focused on the co-occurrence of key words, in an attempt to reveal the relations between them, and to test relational hypotheses. (This is similar to the analytical process in the coding strategy of searching for and analyzing patterns in the occurrence of codes to test hypothetical relations between categories.) As Wood (1984, p. 293) notes, KWIC facilities are necessary where 'the investigator seeks to identify the profile of words appearing in context - that is, "associated" - with a target word or symbol'. As such, KWIC is a vital tool for any kind of contingency analysis, where the researcher aims to infer the network of a source's associations from the pattern of co-occurrences of symbols in messages (Krippendorff, 1980). Furthermore, it is via KWIC retrievals that the researcher is able to construct images and portrayals, and to conduct discriminant analyses. It is through such analytical techniques that researchers are able to develop a fuller understanding of the meaning of key words and, by comparing these meanings, reveal what is unique or specific to them. Since KWIC is the major principle underlying FYI, and the typical usage of this software is to search for words of interest, so that they may be retrieved in their original lexical context, and that the focus of analytical attention is the text around key words (and thus the relations between words), this makes a useful tool for content analysis. But it is precisely because this program contrasts with ETHNOGRAPH in this way, in that the latter focuses analytical attention on the proximity of certain codes to other codes and thereby the relations between them, that KWIC lists provide a complementary analytical tool to the coding segments strategy.

More specifically, KWIC lists are useful in the development of analytic categories, which are depicted by codes in the latter strategy. Since they provide an alternative way of getting to know phenomena, or constructing categories and the relations between them, lexical searching strategies may help to counteract some of the problems of the coding strategy. In particular, they may be useful in a preliminary stage to coding, increasing the understanding of the data (as opposed to knowing them only in terms of analytical classifications) before they are classified into rigid categories. For example, having created a thematic code for psychological states of health, we can study root words depicting feelings (upset*, depress* ang*, fear*, anxious*, stress*, cheerful* etc) and explore the potential for more specific categories (positive, negative, passive, active, neutral etc). More generally, by searching for key words in their context, a fuller meaning of categories may be developed which fit the data in their totality: knowledge of the data and categories is not ascribed in the chronological order of the data, as it is with the coding strategy. This helps to avoid the problems experienced with the coding strategy arising when categories become inadequate.

Key Word out of Context (KWOC)

This is where emphasis is upon single words or short strings of characters which are identified in a text, removed from their linguistic context, individually classified and then counted. The 'vocabulary list' produced by FYI provides this facility. It produces a lexical profile of all the words constituting a data document, in the same way that ETHNOGRAPH's code frequency list displays the code profile for each data document.

Before constructing dictionaries or thesauri, it may be desirable to obtain an overview of the type, variety and distribution of words in the data. Indeed, this may be a fruitful provisional step before conceptualizing the data in any way: it may help researchers decide upon how to organize, index or search data, and thereby choose analytical techniques. This is especially important when the volume of text is as large as it is in much ethnographic research. Without such an overview, researchers risk forming 'biased, incomplete and highly selective impressions' (Krippendorff 1980, 121). An overview of the lexical content of text is virtually impossible to achieve without the help of a computer which, quickly and accurately, is able to produce a tally of words alphabetically or in order of their frequency.

These lists also have other uses. First, alphabetical lists are important because they enable researchers to notice and correct typographical errors in the data which are of vital importance in lexical searching strategies. This is slightly different to the coding segments strategy, where typographical errors in the text have no consequences for analysis. But the spelling of codewords is important, however, since misspelt codes, like misspelt words, will not be retrieved. The vocabulary list, like the alphabetical code list, enables researchers to keep spelling in check.

More specifically, since words in the text are the means through which data are assembled with the lexical search strategy, for its efficiency it is vital that spelling in the text is correct. If there are mistakes in the text, when a search for a certain word is undertaken, occurrences where the word is misspelt will not be retrieved and therefore will not be included, thus inhibiting a thorough analysis and threatening the validity of research findings. Since mistakes in spelling are to an extent inevitable, it is important that FYI accommodates this fact so that, firstly, all mistakes may be easily recognized and that, secondly, all mistakes may be easily changed. With FYI, it is possible to change text already in the filing system and then re-index, but it is easiest if all mistakes are located and then changed all at once. This involves changing the text in the original wordprocessing files and then re-indexing them with FYI.

For the same reason, spelling throughout a data document must be consistent for words which may have more than one legitimate spelling (such as 'organisation' or 'organization'). This may prove to be more problematic where fieldwork involves more than one collector of data or writer of fieldnotes (or qualitative data of any sort). Also, caution must be taken during secondary analysis if the material is gathered from a country where the spelling of certain words is different from that familiar to the researcher. For example, as we were British analysts of American data, we had to take this issue into consideration when searching for words, such as 'centre' and 'colour', which appear as 'center' and 'color' in Roth's fieldnotes.

A similar problem occurs with punctuation marks because FYI treats them as characters and therefore requires their specification in a search. This can be rectified regarding the distinction between upper and lower case letters as FYI can convert all text to upper case. However, regarding punctuation marks, such as apostrophes and hyphens, there is nothing we can do except be aware that they may be interfering with our search. For example, there may be words that are inconsistently hyphenated in the fieldnotes (cooperation may sometimes appear as co-operation) and these will be treated by the computer as different words. However, these types of problems may to a large extent be minimized by consulting the vocabulary list and thereby being aware of the variation of the word of interest. Furthermore, this awareness may be incorporated into a search so that the target be retrieved more efficiently. FYI allows researchers to conduct truncated word searches, which is useful when variations of the word, which may also be of interest, cannot be predicted or guaranteed.

In addition to checking for spelling mistakes, vocabulary lists which include word frequencies are important because, as noted by Wood (1984, p. 292), they draw attention to words which are used either frequently, on the one hand, or infrequently, on the other. This may yield surprising results. For example, in the analysis of a sample of Roth's fieldnotes, 'conflict' had the surprizingly low frequency of 4 whereas 'floor' had the unexpectedly high frequency of 45 (although this makes sense when we consider that fieldnotes are about concrete things rather than general issues). Wood argues that analytical attention must be drawn to the frequency of words while concentrating on aspects of content and style. Otherwise, those words which are used infrequently, but which may be important for understanding a text, may be overlooked. Equally, if attention is not drawn to those words which are used very frequently, researchers risk overlooking the obvious. Also, as Wood (1984, p. 293) argues: '[a]n awareness and notation of rarely used or commonly used words can prove especially useful when one compares texts or speakers'. Such a comparison will obviously involve using the KWOC facility to search for the same words in their original context. However, the fact that FYI attaches frequency values to the alphabetical list (rather than producing a list in order of frequency) may be found to be a disadvantage to researchers who are interested in the relative distribution of key words throughout the text (i.e. if particular key words were selected rather than, as in the case of this research, all words being treated as key words).

Thus, in sum, FYI provides an alphabetical list of key words, or the whole vocabulary, of a given text, with an optional count of each word. Such a list is useful in various ways. First, it seems that reading through the vocabulary list increases familiarity with the diversity of data, since the potential usefulness of words, in terms of phenomena they may indicate, and ideas that develop about the relations between words and phenomena, are noted at a subconscious level. This activity serves as an important preliminary to searching and retrieving data as it provides analytical activity with some direction. However, it may also have negative aspects. Analytic activity based solely on KWOC lists may impede consequential analyses if assumptions and interpretations are inappropriate. For example, from a KWOC list, it is impossible to recognize the meaning attached to a particular word. Thus, it is necessary to be as explicit and reflective about these decisions as possible.

However, if this consideration is borne in mind, the vocabulary list may encourage activities methodologically preferable to those iniated by the code list. For there is one important way in which the KWOC list in the lexical searching strategy differs from the coding strategy's equivalent: when reading the code list, we never look at a code and wonder about its meaning, because we brought the code into existence in the first place and gave it an appropriate definition. However, where data are recordings of conversations, or documents, part of analysis with the lexical searching strategy will be concerned with clarifying their constitutive terms. This process often begins with analyzing KWOC lists which generates questions about lexical meanings. These ideas are then translated into search strings, and the program produces KWIC lists so that we may explore contextual meanings. Although researchers approach the data in various ways via searches, they continually have to read the data in their original context, because the lexical searching strategy positions the KWIC facility at the centre of analysis. Thus it seems that one implication of this strategy is that researchers are forced to analyze original data more thoroughly.

Key words versus codes

Frequencies of the key words noted in the example above contrast sharply with those of their equivalent codes (CONTAM and FLOOR) using ETHNOGRAPH (which were 30, and 3 respectively). Explanation of such surprizing results may be sought in two ways. First, it may be argued that such discrepancies between the two strategies reflect differences in meaning attached to key words in the data, on the one hand, compared with meaning attached to codes as defined by the organizing system, on the other. Put simply, the two strategies seem to retrieve different aspects of the data: the lexical content of what is said as opposed to the semantic content of what is meant (as defined by the analyst). For example, the coding approach draws our attention to topics, rather than specific words, so that 'floor' is coded only so far as it is a topic (such as how it is conceptualized as dirty or clean), rather than simply every time the word is used. In other words, codes are derived from a specific interpretation of the text about its meaning, whereas key words are derived from their literal occurrence in the text itself.

Alternatively, we can ask what conditioned our expectations? Was it a result of observing code frequencies and the amount of text that was retrieved via codes? It is likely that the knowledge gained through using ETHNOGRAPH suggested that these topics were more or less dominant than they appear to be in FYI's representation of the data. If so, it is necessary to consider how different the analysis would have been if it had begun with using FYI as opposed to ETHNOGRAPH. (This question was of course addressed in relation to our own research. The findings about the differences of software reported in this book are, to some extent, contingent upon the order in which we approached the software. Thus it is likely that potentially important methodological issues were not uncovered because of this dependency.) In our experience, the order in which strategies are utilized is important since, when using the lexical searching strategy for the first time, we found it difficult to adjust to this new way of analyzing the data: our thinking was largely bound by the experience of coding.

The representation of data.

As already noted, FYI uses the term 'hit' to describe the retrieved text because it contains the key word targeted in a search. When setting up a filing system, the researcher defines the boundaries of hits, i.e. how much text will be retrieved with the key word. More importantly, the definition of a hit determines what text is relevant to a Boolean search by defining the point at which the proximity of key words to each other in the text ceases to be of significance. The most commonly used option here is the paragraph, since it defines a meaning unit which may be understood by itself. However, this option demands that the fieldnotes are structured in a particular way.

As we encountered with ETHNOGRAPH, the amount of contextual information retrieved with the target code or word is very important for the understanding of the text. This is perhaps even more true of the lexical searching strategy since, unlike the meaning of codes which is defined by the analyst, the meaning of words is indexical or dependent upon the social context in which they are uttered or written. In ethnography, this social context is then reconstructed by the researcher in the ethnographic text, represented in the textual context of the key word. Thus the textual context of a word is vital for the understanding of that word, and any boundaries attached to this context must be flexible.

In contrast to ETHNOGRAPH, where boundaries of segments are fixed, FYI neither requires nor defines contextual boundaries, as such. For although the hit is in the first instance equal to a paragraph, researchers can then 'browse', in either direction from the paragraph, to reveal more of the text. It is useful when large amounts of context are necessary for the interpretation of a segment of text or word, or if the text is structured so that paragraphs or sections cannot be analyzed as if they were relatively independent of each other. However, where a text has little structure in terms of its organization around topics, ideas or events, FYI has more negative implications. The fact that a hit is defined by the paragraph containing the target word results in difficulties where paragraphs are large aggregates of disjointed or disconnected information (although this problem is alleviated with those lexical search programs that highlight the key word in text retrievals). This fact detracts from the focusing of attention and therefore, to some extent, undermines the purpose of the searching process. Similarly, the fact that we are able to browse freely around the text surrounding a hit, may lead us to lose sight of the text originally retrieved in the search, and become 'lost in co-text', so to speak. Again, this may have both positive and negative effects, depending on the style and purpose of research: whether it is to test previously constructed hypotheses, or for a more creative end. In any case, this characteristic of FYI encourages dialogues with the data that are much closer to hypertext trails, than searching for and retrieving coded segments.

The muliplicity of meanings attached to words can be a source of either enlightenment or frustration for those working with the lexical searching strategy. If variations in the meanings attached to words are of interest to researchers, FYI is a very useful tool. With ease, we are able to gather all instances where the term 'bug' is mentioned, to investigate the various meanings that actors bring to this word. For example, we examine the various ways that the movement of bugs are conceptualized, by searching for those instances of the word that appear with 'crawling', 'drifting', or 'flying'. Once we have collated the text relevant to these respective conceptualizations, we can then look for patterns in the characterizations of the movement of bugs as related to the division of labour or other contextual factors. Conversely, we could ask whether some people never use the word at all: we could search for all instances where 'bug' does not occcur in the same paragraph as the name of a particular doctor, for example. Again these kinds of processes parallel those of the coding strategy, in the search for confirming and disconfirming evidence. The difference, of course, is that the lexical searching strategy targets what people actually say, rather than to what they refer or allude, or to what they mean in terms of categories created by analysts.

But for researchers using the lexical searching strategy for other analytical purposes, the multiple meanings of words can prove to be problematic. This is particularly the case, if they are using FYI as a complementary tool for the coding strategy, or to test analytic categories constructed during the coding process, as opposed to the lexical searching technique. For, even in standard English, many words have multiple meanings, and this results in the retrieval of irrelevant portions of text, which confuse or obstruct this process, due to inappropriate meanings being attached to words. This will become clearer with an example.

Having established a preliminary set of categories in the coding process, we may want to test the validity of our categories by testing their fit to data, or explore the plausibility of splitting categories by applying provisional subcategories to data and seeing if they fit. The lexical search strategy provides a relatively quick and easy way of doing this, by selecting a list of synonyms or near-synonyms which approximate the content of the category of interest, from the vocabulary (or KWOC) list. Thus, we may decide that the category of 'conflict' (the hostility which arises during or after a confrontation of opposed interests or antagonistic goals) occurs too frequently to be analytically fruitful: it needs to be more specific in that its definition needs to be narrowed, or subcategories which focus on specific aspects of conflict need to be invented. We may begin by listing all the words which may point to different types and manifestations of conflict, the conditions of these types of conflict, how conflict is controlled, and so on (figure 3.1).

Thesaurus for conflict

ACCUS*	CURS*	RILED
ANG*	CRUEL	SHOUT*
ANTAG*	DISAGREE*	STIR*
ARGU*	DEFEN*	TROUBL*
BATTL*	FIGHT*	UPSET*
BAWL*	HOSTIL*	UNCOOPERAT*
BITCH*	INSULT*	UNFAIR*
BLAB*	OBJECT*	UNPARDONABLE
BLAM*	MAD*	UNREASONABL*
COMPETIT*	PUNISH*	VIOLEN*
CONTEMPT*	REFUS*	WRONG*
CRITIC*		

Figure 3.1 A list of synonyms and near-synonyms of conflict

Theoretically, we may then divide these synonyms into groups, such as conditions, strategies, consequences. This is not an easy task because the meanings of terms are of course context-dependent. But if we believed it possible to do this, given our familiarity with the data, a search can then be conducted on each group of words, by arranging them into a search string using the 'or' operator. By examining the text retrieved in such searches, we may then decide whether splitting the code for conflict into three more specific ones is justified, or if they fit the data. On the contrary, we may find that this way of recontextualizing the data suggests that the new categories are superfluous, or the distinctions between them superficial.

If, however, researchers use words (like codes) as search terms to access phenomena, there is an underlying assumption that they have a relationship to those phenomena. The multiple meanings of words proves to undermine such assumptions. In looking for text relevant to manifestations of conflict, a search will be made on a selection of key words taken from our list of synonyms, but not all text retrieved will be relevant to conflict. Figure 3.2 shows one example. In this instance, 'object' was used as one of the synonyms for conflict, but here it means a 'physical entity', not the verb 'to oppose or argue'.

The predictability of the meanings attached to words, and thereby the relevance of text retrieved in searches on those words, is not only confused by words that generally have multiple meanings. In interview transcripts, for example, people might use certain words idiosyncratically, or in ways that seem out of context to the researcher. In any case, the lexical search program must enable the researcher to siphon the retrieved text in some way: in order to maximize the relevance of all printed (or filed) material, we must be able to edit search results, or 'mark' hits, to eliminate unwanted information. Arguably, editing capabilities are more important with lexical search software than they are with coding software. For although ETHNOGRAPH allows the researcher to edit the search, this function is less likely to be as necessary since the text which is significant to a particular topic, theme, or phenomenon has in effect already been selected as such through the coding process.

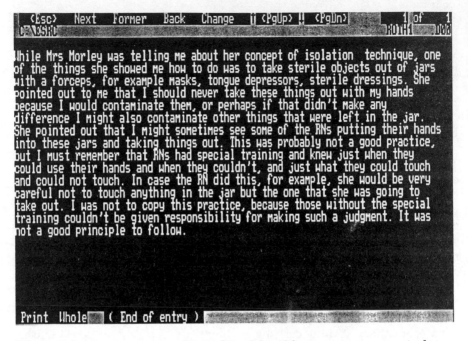

Figure 3.2   An FYI screen. Data found by this program are not always relevant to the searched for concept: this text bears no relevance to the analytical topic 'conflict'.

But, the problems associated with the inability to predict the meanings of words do not only necessitate particular technical requirements of lexical search programs: more fundamentally, they question the epistemological grounds of using the lexical searching strategy to test or develop coding techniques. It certainly is questionable from a poststructuralist position, where the meanings associated with words are not inherent to themselves, but depend on contexts of other words which, in turn, depend on further contexts in a process of differing and deferring which can only be arbitrarily halted (Derrida, 1982). It seems that it is precisely these processes that should be the focus of lexical searching techniques.

Types of data and types of analysis.

The merits of the lexical searching strategy are obviously not universal: they vary with types of data to be analyzed, and types of analytic goals (for example, if it is used to complement coding, why, and when). Thus it is necessary for researchers to reflect on the type of data in their research, and what exactly they want to do with them. Only then can the lexical searching strategy be appreciated in context. This context is methodologically important because it affects the researcher's choice of analytical strategies and tools. For this reason, it is necessary to make explicit the methodological context of the research upon which this book is based.

Our research was based on a set of ethnographic fieldnotes, thus it is necessary to think about the nature of these data, and how amenable they are to lexical analysis. First, the lexical searching strategy is clearly useful if we want to locate material things in the data, such as particular pieces of medical equipment, or specific persons. The advantages are not quite so obvious regarding exploring concepts and the meanings with which people make sense of their everyday lives. One reason for this is that this is that, in our research, the data consisted of what Roth wrote. If we were working with interview transcripts or other documents, on the other hand, then the significance of what is actually said may be greater (or at least different).

Second, fieldnotes are not simply recordings of reality, since much interpretation on the part of the researcher is inscribed in writing fieldnotes. As Atkinson (1990, p. 61) notes, despite the imagery of 'writing down' what goes on (which implies that the transcription of reality is uninterrupted by self-conscious intervention or reflection), writing fieldnotes is a matter of textual construction. Although fieldnotes are often treated as 'data' in the analytical and 'writing up' phases of research, in that they are the bases upon which inferences and knowledge are built, they themselves are narratives which portray transactions and reflections of field experience, dialogues with the self, observations and inferences. (The 'reality' is deferred.)

This certainly characterizes Roth's fieldnotes. These fieldnotes are not simply a record of empirical observation since they reflect his role as social participant as well as data collector. He adds meaning to his experiences and observations much in the same way as the other participants in the field, only he has to be explicitly aware of the knowledge and cultural assumptions through which he constructs his 'cognitive map' of reality. Roth's fieldnotes reflect these activities so that empirical observations are interjected with attempts to understand or explain what he has seen by relating it to other incidents in the field, and to experiences and knowledge external to the field.

This nature of ethnographic fieldnotes has implications for the analytical strategy adopted. At the outset, it would seem that it renders the lexical searching strategy less useful than in other types of textual analysis. Since the exact words and ideas expressed by participants in the field only constitute a small part of the text, the words of the text (which are the tools of analysis using the lexical searching strategy), belong to the author of the text. Likewise, the ideas and interpretations to be searched and analyzed are likely to be those of the ethnographer, as opposed to those of the people of interest. For example, a search on 'conflict' in Roth's fieldnotes will result in the retrieval of a 'voice' which is distinctly that of the researcher, such as:

This conflict between shifts and the griping about the other one's laziness is a common feature of hospitals.

The event preceding this sentence in the fieldnotes is classified as 'conflict' by Roth (not necessarily by those directly involved in the event) who then proceeds to generalize this event as a common type of conflict. Take another example:

This kind of conflict is likely to be reflected in the care of the patients in the future. When Morley calls for something from the kitchen, she's less likely to get good service than she would if she were on good terms with the kitchen workers. The patients might suffer by getting the wrong kind of food or having to wait a long time before getting some dish they asked for.

Again, it is Roth who is hypothesizing here. This characteristic of fieldnotes may prove to be rather confusing to researchers using the lexical searching strategy, if they want to examine how actors themselves define and deal with conflict. And if researchers are unaware of any such interference, this ultimately will have implications for the validity of their research.

Indeed, it seems that lexical searching strategies are most suited to types of research which evaluate verbal or textual communication, focusing on what people say and the way that they say it. It is in these types of research that content analysis is more employable. Of course, in order to study how reality is constructed through speech or writing, the data must have a certain quality. Clearly, if we want to discover how meanings (values, norms, intentions etc) are inscribed in lexicons, and how these guide action (as embodied in the text), fieldnotes are inappropriate. Rather, 'data' are interview transcriptions (in the case sociological research) or documents of interest (as in the case of historical research or cultural studies). In such cases, it is the meaning systems of the authors of documents, and the way they are implied in communication, which are being scrutinized. This also applies to unstructured qualitative research since the actors themselves are to some extent the authors of interview transcripts.

By contrast, the ethnographer will generally not show such a degree of interest in the author of the fieldnotes because the author and analyst tend to be the same person. But this is not always the case. Many years after conducting their research, researchers may revisit their data, and here they will seem as much a textual construct as the other people and events described in the fieldnotes (Atkinson, 1992). In such circumstances, they might want to rediscover how certain conclusions were reached, or place their ideas under new scrutiny. Indeed, this is a consequence of the increasing tendency for researchers to be reflexive about their research. We constantly need to be aware of our role and status as authors, and it seems that the lexical searching strategy will be invaluable for this purpose.

In both of these cases, the experiences of the ethnographer in the field may be intentionally used as data in themselves, rather than being repressed or swept away with other redundant material. For example, since Roth covertly negotiated access to his field by being employed as a hospital attendant, the descriptions and reflections about his personal experience in the field which shape the fieldnotes may be used as data about the experience of being a hospital attendant or, more specifically, being socialized into this new role. Or, as secondary analysts, we might want to examine how Roth textually reconstructs a medical setting, by examining the lexical content, structure and style of his work, comparing the fieldnotes with his research papers and monograph. In all of these examples of the ways in which the author (or authoring) of a document may be of interest to qualitative researchers, the lexical searching strategy is invaluable.

In addition to types of data and types of analysis, the structure of the data also has important consequences for analysis using the lexical searching strategy. Data are structured in various ways, usually for practical reasons. In interviews, a new paragraph often signifies speech uttered by different person. There are similar narrative techniques in ethnographic fieldnotes. For example, there is a tendency for researchers to structure the text in a way that helps to differentiate between the narration of events, on the one hand, and the researcher's 'voice', which attempts to reflect and comment on such events in the fieldnotes, on the other. This is so it remains clear whose opinion is being expressed. However, if the structural distinction between the two voices in the text is made via paragraphs, the two voices will be defined as separate 'hits'.

Take the following segment of text from Roth's fieldnotes which is defined as a hit by FYI because it constitutes a paragraph:

> This conflict between shifts and the griping about the other one's laziness and good-for-nothingness is a common feature of hospitals.

Clearly, this comment cannot be understood in isolation. The previous paragraph, which describes the social event that is identified as conflict in Roth's comment above, is of vital importance to an analysis of conflict, but it was not retrieved in this search because it lay outside the 'hit'. Researchers therefore have to browse the co-text of this segment to see the evidence or motivation of Roth's generalization about conflict. Fortunately, this is not a problem when searching for text and analyzing results on the computer screen, because FYI allows us to browse around hits with ease. However, it is more of a problem if we want to print text retrieved in a search automatically. (Indeed, it seems that FYI is most effective for analysis when used online, whereas with ETHNOGRAPH it makes no difference.) Thus, when deciding how to define hits, researchers must consider how different voices are structurally distinguished in the text. The use of brackets or other symbols may be more appropriate than separate paragraphs for this purpose.

The most striking difference between the methodological demands of the coding segments and lexical searching strategies is regarding data preparation. The whole process of coding constitutes essential data preparation, as without this stage, the search facilities of ETHNOGRAPH cannot be utilized. Thinking of the coding process as data preparation encourages the recognition of its effect of shaping the data, or adding to it a structure that suits the interests of a particular piece of research. Furthermore, this structure demands that we have thorough knowledge of the data so that coding may be adequate. All this amounts to the fact that, by the time researchers reach the search and retrieval stage, they will already be familiar with the data, and that their activities during this phase will be guided and structured by decisions that were made earlier, on the basis of this knowledge. The centrality of this phase of analysis is to some extent displaced by the coding process.

The implication is that knowledge acquisition in the coding segments strategy is to a large extent predetermined by the linear structure of the text (as represented in the original fieldnotes). This influence on the results of analysis raises questions about the validity of the coding segments strategy. FYI, however, does not make these demands on researchers, so avenues of analysis are much less predetermined. With FYI, it is only via the process of searching and retrieving data that knowledge is able to accumulate. Analysis via searching may begin at any point in the document, unlike the process of coding which begins at the beginning of the text and ends at the end, along with the knowledge that accompanies this experience.

Since analysis is far less predetermined by the linearity of the text, or by predefined chronological stages, search and retrieval with the lexical searching strategy is much more flexible and exploratory than with the coding segments strategy. Researchers can follow up any whim or idea spontaneously, rather than search for only those which have been already anticipated (to some extent). Furthermore, the distinct lack of data categorization removes the possibility of problems resulting from the latter being inaccurate. At the stage of retrieval and analysis, every word in the text has the potential to be significant to the analytic search: no analytic avenues are prematurely closed. To be used effectively for qualitative analysis, FYI requires researchers to use the lexical searching technique to gain knowledge of the data, and as a basis upon which to structure analysis. Definition of structure is concurrent with analysis rather than a preliminary to it.

However, this lack of structure can have the effect of making researchers feel lost, or not know where to begin. Faced with this situation, researchers familiar with the coding strategy may use this way of approaching data as a basis of structuring analysis with a lexical search program (i.e constructing thesauri to represent categories). However, even for this purpose, this strategy has a distinct advantage over ETHNOGRAPH: it continues to be flexible throughout the whole process of analysis. By analyzing the vocabulary list and the content of searches on words of interest, the researcher is able to create dictionaries and thesauri to classify the text and open up new paths of inquiry. Using the search technique in this way is likely to avoid the problems which arise when researchers want to approach the text in a different way, in line with their changing understanding of the text. Changes which occur in the way data are conceptualized may be easily accommodated, because the text itself is not actually structured by FYI; rather, researchers use FYI to structure their approach to the text (i.e. in a search string).

Since the lexical searching strategy retains a dynamic representation of the text and is a more flexible way for the researcher to deepen their understanding of the text, it may be productive to combine it with more inflexible approaches (which have other advantages) for a more thorough analysis. For example, it may be possible that KWIC lists, thesauri, dictionaries and the like may be, firstly, a useful preliminary to the construction of categories of meaning as required by the coding strategy or, secondly, to cross-validate findings obtained by the coding segments technique. The fact that no data preparation is necessary for FYI renders the combining of strategies practically, as well as methodologically, plausible.

Volume, diversity and focus

Searches on codes with ETHNOGRAPH, and their lexical equivalents with FYI, produce very different results in terms of the amount of data retrieved. For example, in our research, the search on conflict with FYI produced much more data than did ETHNOGRAPH. Since such a large list of synonyms or near-synonyms had been constructed for conflict, there were many ways in which the researcher was able to access the data. In fact, this search strategy produced too much data to analyze in any systematic way and thus was inefficient for our given purpose. This is in contrast to the amount of data produced by ETHNOGRAPH which appeared to be much more focused. Indeed, researchers were able to anticipate, when stipulating a search on the code for conflict, the data that would be retrieved. This is because the phenomenon of interest had already been predefined in the coding process, and thus only instances relevant to this definition were retrieved. Whether data were included in or excluded from a search on conflict ultimately depended upon the definition of conflict.

In the early stages of the coding process, we defined 'conflict' as follows:

> The hostility which arises during or after a confrontation of opposed interests or antagonistic goals. Conflict is related to noncooperation and inflexibility, and usually occurs in the context of staff relations, patient-staff relations, staff deviance, patient deviance, and the division of labour.

This definition was designed to be open enough to embrace as of yet invisible aspects of the phenomenon, so that via the search process researchers would be able to see more than could the naked eye, or the reader of fieldnotes, and thus obtain a deeper understanding of conflict. On the other hand, such a definition was needed to guide the coding process and make the search as focused as possible, so that all the material retrieved is relevant to the researcher's interests. This maximizes the power of researchers to recognize new aspects of the phenomenon uncovered by the search. Although, this ideal balance is very difficult to achieve in practice, a search with ETHNOGRAPH produces a coherent body of material which is amenable to systematic analysis, because it is to some extent prescribed by decisions made in the coding process.

By contrast, a search on conflict using FYI is not prescribed by decisions made earlier in the research process and, as a result of this lack of constraints, analysts are much freer to tip the balance in either direction. However, the crucial difference here is that, if a search is not successful, researchers may choose from an almost infinite range of alternatives how to make it more successful. Any word, or combination of words, in the text may spontaneously be evoked to attempt to penetrate the intended subject matter, since following up a 'hunch' needs no preparation, and has no organizational consequences for the rest of analysis. Also, changes of analytical direction or focus may easily be accommodated by FYI, because it does not rely upon a specific way of organizing the text, but simply a way of approaching it.

Thus, an apparent failure to produce a useful search on conflict with FYI does not, in itself, make the strategy of searching for coded segments superior to that of lexical searching: disadvantages due to the lack of structure in this analytical strategy may be easily rectified. Paradoxically, this lack of structure may in itself be enough for some researchers to argue for FYI's superiority given the value attached to flexibility in qualitative methodology. In any case, this lack of structure in the search and analysis phase may have other advantages over the more structured approach embodied in the coding segments strategy.

First, it is possible that FYI's lack of structural demands enhances the capacity of this tool to provide insights to more subtle and implicit aspects and processes. For example, in the analysis of conflict, it seemed that not only did FYI retrieve paragraphs where conflict was the object of description or discussion (which were recognized by the researcher in the coding process and thus also retrieved with ETHNOGRAPH), but also those instances where manifestations of conflict are less obvious so they had not been observed during the coding process. Conflict may often remain hidden so that the only way of identifying its presence is through its expression in certain words. Looking at the context in which words such as 'bitch', 'blab', 'anger', 'hostile', and 'violent' appear, may provide important insights to the conflictual undercurrents of social action which otherwise would not have been observed.

Evidence for this is found in the fact that, in our search on conflict, not all those segments of text retrieved by FYI were retrieved by ETHNOGRAPH: effects of the lexical searching strategy suggested that much more text was relevant to this topic. This is because, during the coding process, these data did not fit our definition of the category 'conflict'. Take the following excerpt from the fieldnotes found in FYI's search on our thesaurus for conflict (because of the word 'uncooperative'), but not retrieved in ETHNOGRAPH's representation of this category:

> The question came up during the day about whether they should feel sorry for Mr Linn because he was locked up and because he had a lot of problems on the outside and had been a mental patient and whether they should take all those things into consideration when thinking about how uncooperative he had been. Hodge said she had felt very sorry for him when he first came in here, but after he had escaped three times and had to be dragged back and locked up she finally got a little bit fed up with it. She's through being sorry for him. A man like that has to be controlled. When Lovell came around, she mentioned that he had been classified as a schizophrenic which was the worst kind of mental disease. This seemed to impress Walters quite a bit and she was now convinced that her fears about him 'being wild' were justified and agreed that a man like that had to be restrained even though it did seem inhuman to some extent.

This event does not so much display manifestations or signs of contradictory interests as much as conflictual conditions experienced by one person, or a group of people. It depicts the role conflict experienced by these people as nurses or attendants with specific interests and duties, on the one hand, and as morally sensitive and responsible human beings, on the other. This kind of conflict is not made obvious by the semantics of the text. But by focusing on the lexical content of the segment, this particular interpretation comes to light more easily. Seen in this way, the segment shows a symptom or side effect of role conflict: the articulation of potentially uncomfortable moral issues. It also shows how the harmful potential of these are dissolved: they are subordinated to processes of rationalization; the patient's behaviour is seen as abnormal so that normal standards of humanity need not apply. In this instance, nurses see their action as necessary rather than as immoral, and in this way role conflict is diffused.

Thus it may be concluded that the lexical searching strategy provides a more diverse and flexible representation of data, which is less subject to the linearity of data, yields less predictable results, and therefore is perhaps more useful a tool for exploration and enlightenment than is searching for coded segments. It is also less mechanical, in that we do not feel compelled to conduct searches without first considering their analytical worth. (From our experience, the only way that mechanical activity may characterize the research process is if it is used as a method for testing ideas emergent from the coding process.) Researchers are encouraged to scroll text, and edit searches before printing output, so they are less likely to generate redundant piles of recontextualized data. However, the effectiveness of the lexical searching strategy is contingent on the adequacy of thesauri and dictionaries prepared by researchers which guide the search process. Moreover, this chapter suggests that it depends very much on the nature of data and the aims of research - in particular whether it is used as a strategy in its own right, or to complement coding. The next chapter takes some of the issues associated with combining coding and lexical searching a stage further, by looking at a program designed specifically for grounded theory that attempts to integrate both.

4 Coding and theory building

Introduction

This chapter will discuss briefly two programs: KWALITAN, created by Peters and Wester in the Netherlands; and NUDIST, designed by Richards and Richards in Australia. These two programs appear in a chapter of their own because they do not fit neatly into any of the general strategies - coding, lexical searching, or hypertext - discussed in this book. Yet neither do they represent an alternative strategy in themselves. For although KWALITAN and NUDIST employ a general coding approach, they provide other facilities in addition: NUDIST supports lexical searching, and both enable researchers to annotate data, define concepts, and write memos without having to leave the program (and data therein). From this, it can be argued that such programs actually transform the conventional copy-and-paste method, as exemplified by ETHNOGRAPH. More specifically, rather than being tools for simply organizing data into thematic categories, these programs support activities intrinsic to theory building, or versions of analysis conforming to the 'Grounded Theory' tradition.

Excluding articles written by the authors of these programs (for example, Richards and Richards, 1987, 1991a and b), the attention received by them in methodological discourse is still rather sparse. For example, in the most extensive guide to software for qualitative research (Tesch, 1990), NUDIST is mentioned only in passing, and KWALITAN is not mentioned at all. This is partly because the stand-alone or PC compatible version of the former, and the English language version of the latter, are relatively new products. Independent evaluations are clearly necessary, particularly given their potential for transforming coding as a computer-assisted approach to qualitative analysis. The first part of this chapter will outline the essence of these programs. The second will illustrate, through comparisons with ETHNOGRAPH and other programs, how they transform qualitative analysis from an activity of organizing, summarizing, and searching text, to theorizing about data.

The KWALITAN workfile

Before KWALITAN can be used for analysis, there are several steps researchers must undertake to prepare data. First, ASCII files (exported from a word processor) must be transformed into 'raw data files'. This basically involves inserting the identification and description of the file (such as 'Roth3a: Week 3, day 1') into a specific position in the text, and dividing the document into 'scenes' or 'units of analysis'. At this point, no segments of data may be omitted from the raw document file: all text must be included in scenes. Furthermore, data can belong to one scene only: scenes are not permitted to overlap. (Both of these conditions do not apply later, when the scene structure can be modified.) Researchers may also add a keyword to all

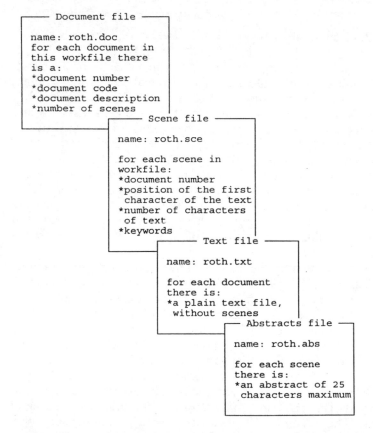

Figure 4.1 The structure of a KWALITAN workfile (adapted from Peters and Wester, 1990, p. 60)

or some of the scenes at this stage if desired. The data files are then ready to be read by KWALITAN.

The researchers' task is then to create a 'workfile', which is like a catalogue or directory, into which the data documents are to be placed. Once researchers have specified a name for the workfile (Roth), KWALITAN automatically creates a workfile. This consists of four different files which focus on different types of information about the data (figure 4.1). As the raw documents are read into the empty workfile, these files are automatically updated. They function to enable researchers to obtain information easily about the scene structure of a document, and to retrieve the abstracts and raw text of its scenes. Once the workfile is complete, analysis with KWALITAN may begin. With this program, analysis consists of: first, browsing data by navigating between scenes; second, redefining scenes in line with emerging conceptualization; and third, attaching up to ten keywords (each consisting of up to twenty characters) to scenes. Subsequently, researchers may explore the data either by browsing or by displaying specific instances in the data by specifying the keywords, scenes, or documents to be searched. The process of segmenting the data into scenes and applying keywords is much quicker than with ETHNOGRAPH, since coding is applied directly - online - rather than in two stages. Likewise, researchers can modify both the scene structure and keywords with ease, at any point in analysis.

Memo files

Researchers may also attach up to four types of memo files to the workfile, each designed for a distinct purpose. First, there is a file containing 'profile cards'. Here, a profile card may be completed for each data document, including descriptive information about the particular case, or the conditions of the field from which the data are taken, or whatever constitute the 'research units'. These serve a similar function to facilities termed 'face-sheets' or 'headers' in other programs. For example, in our research on Roth's fieldnotes, we could use a profile card for each day of data, and include the ward in which he was working during that day, and even the personnel who were working the same shift. Second, there is a memo file containing 'concept cards' which focus on information about keywords and the concepts which develop during analysis. As discussed in the second chapter of this book, the process of defining and redefining concepts in analysis was an essential activity, and this facility in KWALITAN recognizes and encourages it as such. Third, there is a file consisting of theoretical memos, where researchers may store the thoughts and hypotheses arising during analysis which contribute to theory development. Fourth, researchers may write comments about the way in which data collection and analyses have been achieved in a file containing method memos (Peters and Wester, 1990, p. 56). In all of these cases, fleeting ideas are more likely to be recorded and therefore followed up. Furthermore, since definitions, propositions and other products of analysis are spatially closer to data - in that they reside in the same database - it is likely that there will more interaction between them. Finally, memo files do not have to be specific to a particular workfile: they are independent from, and can be attached to a number of workfiles. Thus the same memoranda may be attached to several research projects, or data sets which may facilitate research incorporating cross-site analysis, or exploring patterns between different cases.

NUDIST

The name of this program, which stands for 'Non-numerical Unstructured Data Indexing, Searching and Theorizing' (Richards et al, 1990a, p. 2), suggests several things about its assumptions. First, it suggests something about the kind of data to be analyzed by the program. Since data are defined as 'non-numerical' rather than textual, this implies that NUDIST supports broader qualitative research than do most programs. There has been a tendency for coding programs to support the analysis of text only, whereas this one encourages researchers to analyze material such as photographs and music as well as text using the microcomputer. Second, the program's name suggests something about the kinds of tasks for which it is designed to support: with NUDIST, analysis consists of indexing, searching, and theorizing about data.

Conceptually, NUDIST consists of two databases: one containing the data themselves (fieldnotes, interview transcripts, diaries etc. - i.e. data documents), and one *about* the data (the index system). Figure 4.2 shows the conceptual relations between the different elements of NUDIST.

The document system

The document system contains online documents (such as fieldnotes) and references to offline documents (such as newspaper cuttings), as well as information about these documents (analytical notes). For either type of document to be included in the system, they first have to be divided into 'text units'. With online (word-processed) documents, 'raw' (ASCII) data files, this is an equivalent process to defining 'segments' with ETHNOGRAPH or, more closely, 'scenes' with KWALITAN. With an offline newspaper article, each subheading may signify a new text unit. By default, the program treats each paragraph as a separate text unit. If researchers are happy with this way of demarcating text, raw data files need no preparation whatsoever and can be read directly into NUDIST. However, researchers can customize the format of their data to suit their needs if they are not satisfied with this arrangement. Since the program treats each hard carriage return as a new text unit, these can be inserted into the relevant places of the ASCII files, before they are integrated into a NUDIST project. In this way, text units may constitute sentences or lines of text for a more fine-grained analysis.

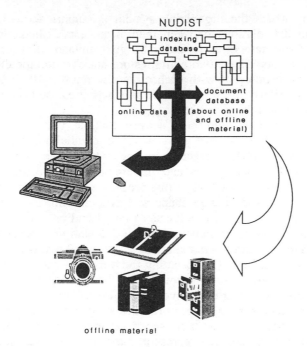

Figure 4.2   The conceptual structure of NUDIST (adapted from Richards and Richards et al., 1990a, p. 12)

NUDIST's in-built assumption that not all sources of information relevant to a research project can or need to be online is indeed innovative in itself: researchers are invited to store information about these sources in NUDIST so that computer-assisted analysis may expand to include this realm of data as well as online text. However, it also has another implication: data do not have to be textual to be an integral part of analysis. Files representing offline data are defined into one or more units of analysis. For example, a photograph may be defined as a whole unit, and each entry in a respondent's diary may constitute a separate text unit. This enables offline data to be indexed in the same way as online data, and thus be included in a search. When researchers want to review all information that is relevant to a certain category, NUDIST will also tell them a bit about relevant sources that lie outside the computer, where to find them, etc. The only difference between online and offline data documents is that only the former can be retrieved in a full text search.

The index system

The index system lies at the heart of analysis with NUDIST. To work, the system requires two kinds of activity. First, it involves 'node building'. This is the means by which the organizing system is constructed, or analytic categories - and the relations between them - are established. Second, it involves using these categories to index the text units of both online and offline data documents. These two activities are not chronologically related however: they are concurrent with each other and ongoing throughout the whole analysis. Similarly, they are not the sole activities: both interact with strategies of lexical searching and browsing.

NUDIST's index system represents a very flexible way of organizing documents - both online and offline - in terms of analytic categories. It works on the principle that, as researchers become familiar with their data, they construct analytic categories and hierarchical relationships between them. An analogous representation of this process would be a group of trees that continually grow and change shape and become enmeshed with each other. Each tree consists of various levels of nodes and branches; the nodes represent categories and the branches represent the relations between them.

By analogy, a NUDIST index system is like an upside-down tree. At the top is the trunk, or a single node (representing the most general or fundamental category). As we move down through the tree, branches and nodes (representing more specific or exclusive categories and the relations between them) become more numerous. A tree provides an ideal way of representing variables that constitute a hierarchical social structure. For example, in the analysis of Roth's data, one tree represented the occupational hierarchy in the TB hospital, and its nodes represented the various positions of social roles within this hierarchy.

More abstractly, a tree may be used to represent an analytic theme, with its contained nodes being the topics encompassed by the theme. Figure 4.3 shows one possibility: the whole tree is concerned with ideas about contamination or, more specifically, the ideas that are enshrined in a set of rules that seek to control contamination ('isolation technique'). In this tree, branches represent different types of ideas about contamination. For example, all data indexed with the node address 1 1 1 1 1 are concerned with rules that seek to prevent the contamination of persons by bugs, which are seen as agents of contamination. By contrast, all data indexed with the node 1 1 2 2 2 are concerned with rules that seek to cure (or 'clean') the environment from inorganic substances or dirt.

In the course of a project, nodes and even collections of nodes (subtrees) invariably will need to be moved or deleted. Such changes to the index system are easily accommodated by NUDIST. Similarly, new nodes may need to be added to a tree. Node-building is supported throughout the whole of analysis. Although the procedure of building nodes seems to be quite complicated at first, mostly because of the way a node's position or 'address' is depicted (see figure 4.3), hands-on practice solves this very quickly. At any rate, researchers do not need to memorize node addresses: node titles can be used to manipulate data instead (e.g. 1 1 1 2 2 = contaminat/ isolat.tech/personal/cure/dirt). Also, NUDIST can list nodes in terms of their titles.

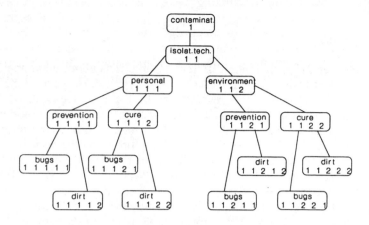

Figure 4.3 A NUDIST subtree, showing how nodes are built into hierarchical structures, and how their 'addresses' reflect their position in the hierarchy.

In addition, NUDIST provides some useful statistics about text searches - whether using lexical criteria, or node combinations. For example, it indicates the percentage of text units, for a document or range of files, containing the search term. ETHNOGRAPH lacks a facility of such sophistication but, as argued in a previous chapter, quantitative information about the way data have been indexed may sometimes be a useful analytic tool in qualitative analysis.

Thus NUDIST is a powerful tool for qualitative analysis - although this is somewhat hindered by its poor interface. For despite being a Windows application, NUDIST contains no pop-up menus, soft buttons or multiple windows, and does not effectively support a mouse. In short, it does not effectively take advantage of Windows' graphical user interface. Rather, text is awkwardly scrolled onto the screen, and there it remains until more text forces it to roll off again. Menus too appear in this way so that, even after a menu option has been specified, it remains on the screen until pushed off by new information.

This proves to be rather frustrating at times, especially when the retrieval of a whole document or a large text unit is required. This is because NUDIST continues to output the whole text, in this scrolling fashion, until it reaches the end. An irreducible necessity of any tool for qualitative analysis is for researchers to be able to scroll through text at their own pace. Instead, NUDIST's reader has to scroll backwards to find the information required. And if the document is longer than a certain number of pages, the user is unable to retrieve its first pages via the scroll bar. These factors make first encounters with NUDIST rather daunting, but they become less of a problem as its assets become more obvious.

Discussion

Defining segments

Both KWALITAN and NUDIST make different assumptions about what analysis is, and the kinds of tasks the analyst will want to pursue. However, both are more similar to each other in this respect than they are to ETHNOGRAPH. For the assumptions of both programs enable them to transcend a model of analysis where text is coded simply for its retrieval. They also transcend rather simplistic types of CAQDAS theory building based on the cooccurrence of codes - a rather weak approach since the cooccurrence of codes does not necessarily imply a relation between variables (Weitzman and Miles, 1994). In sum, both KWALITAN and NUDIST mobilize a combination of aspects of two of the established microcomputing strategies examined in this project: segment coding and hypertext. NUDIST goes even further in crossing boundaries between strategies in that it also provides a comprehensive lexical searching facility specifically geared for theory building in qualitative analysis. The discussion will now turn to a brief comparison of KWALITAN and NUDIST to other programs to illustrate these points.

An essential aspect of analysis with KWALITAN is the segmentation of data into scenes. This, it would seem, is similar to the activity central to ETHNOGRAPH. But there is a difference which lies in their method of decontexualization or, to put it another way, the criteria used when segmenting data. This difference has consequences for the whole nature of analysis. More specifically, what distinguishes these two programs is that, with ETHNOGRAPH, segments of data are individually coded regarding their analytical content. Thus, with the Roth data, fieldnotes are demarcated into segments according to their relevance to thematic categories or topics, such as the attitudes of TB patients toward contamination or the personal management of their disease. The link between such topics and segments is referenced by a code representing the former, consisting of ten characters maximum.

However, it is useful to characterize the conceptual structure of this process regarding both programs to reveal the differences in their approach. With ETHNOGRAPH, the way data are segmented is dependent upon their relevance to analytical categories: having read a paragraph, the researcher first identifies which categories or codes are relevant and then segments the paragraph accordingly. Thus, coding conceptually precedes segmenting. With KWALITAN, however, the structure of this process is turned on its head. The process begins with defining a 'scene', which constitutes a 'unit of analysis' (Peters and Wester, 1990, p. 53). More specifically, scenes consist of 'natural transitions in the data'. These may be separate questions in interview transcripts, or individual paragraphs and passages in ethnographic fieldnotes. Once a scene is defined (by a symbol appearing at its beginning and end), researchers then assign up to ten keywords to characterize it.

NUDIST is similar to KWALITAN in this respect, because tagging the data conceptually succeeds rather than precedes segmenting the data. Data are segmented into 'text units' - usually defined by paragraphs - at the outset. Analysis consists of indexing these units and exploring the indexing system simultaneously. The 'addresses' (code numbers) of index nodes are attached to predefined text units. Like KWALITAN and unlike ETHNOGRAPH, NUDIST defines coding or 'indexing' as an essential part of analysis: it is not relegated to data preparation but rather continues to shape data throughout the whole process.

KWALITAN and NUDIST both give researchers much more control than does ETHNOGRAPH in segmenting data. Both involve entering special symbols into the data to define the beginning and end of segment boundaries. In this way, they are much more flexible than ETHNOGRAPH since it supports no alternative to dividing data into segments other than by lines of text. As discussed in chapter two of this book, line numbers are not an entirely satisfactory method of segmenting fieldnotes. This is because segments rarely begin at the beginning of one line and end at the end of another. Furthermore, with NUDIST, researchers do not have to decide to define all text units of a project as either paragraphs, sentences or lines. This is often useful: if a project consists of different types of data documents (for example fieldnotes, interview transcripts and participant diaries), not all of them can be divided very easily into the same type of text units. Finally, the fact that NUDIST and KWALITAN allow researchers to define their segments according to grammatical units not only contributes to neater retrieval, but also reduces time-consuming preparation, and involves fewer technical problems.

Hierarchical codes

Despite allowing fewer keywords than ETHNOGRAPH permits codes (twelve), there are several advantages of KWALITAN's system of tagging text. These stem from two features. First, that keywords can consist of up to twenty characters and, second, that researchers may specify only part of a keyword to be searched. Conjunctively, these features enable the construction of keywords that are hierarchical (Peter and Wester, 1990, p. 122). We found this to be a very useful feature. When designing an organizing system for codes earlier in the research, we wanted to code data for both very general and very specific categories. It seemed to us that the most obvious way to facilitate this was to use hierarchical codes. These could logically be divided into parts - the first part representing the most abstract or general aspect of the category, and the last part denoting the most specific. For example, moving from the general to the more specific, all the segments of data relevant to hygiene, contamination and bugs would be tagged with a single hierarchical code such as 'hyg contam bug' (rather than three separate ones, which frequently caused many types of problems). Unlike KWALITAN, ETHNOGRAPH does not accommodate hierarchical coding; we consider this to be a considerable shortcoming.

NUDIST's system of coding or indexing also encourages the use of hierarchical categories, in that a node consists of several hierarchical concepts or categories. But whereas KWALITAN's keywords are limited to twenty characters each, NUDIST accommodates much greater complexity: theoretically, there is no limit to the length of a node's title. Of all the programs evaluated so far, NUDIST certainly seems to be the best equipped for organizing data in terms of categories that vary widely in terms of their generality and specificity.

Browsing context

Another apparent advantage of KWALITAN over ETHNOGRAPH, is that it more readily accommodates the likely need to read the text surrounding a particular segment. This is because it identifies the text by automatically numbering scenes (as opposed to numbering lines of text), and because the relevant scene number appears alongside the scene whenever it is displayed, or retrieved in a search for a keyword. This means that, to read surrounding text, researchers simply note the present scene number, and then select to display the preceding or succeeding scene number until all the necessary information has been read. Likewise, easy browsing extends to NUDIST because it automatically numbers text units.

By contrast, with ETHNOGRAPH text is identified by an automatic numbering of lines: the segments themselves do not have a number (they are only defined by the codes that are attached to them). Thus, to display the context of a segment, the researcher has to be able to specify the line numbers of interest. However, this knowledge is not at hand. Besides relying on guess-work, the only alternative would be to display the whole document and then find the location of the target text manually.

Thus KWALITAN and NUDIST encourage strategies of rereading the raw data in its original context more readily than does ETHNOGRAPH. Furthermore, they are more useful tools for 'getting to know the data' and may intervene analysis at a much earlier stage. Researchers may progress from scene to scene, or from one text unit to the next, before data have been tagged in any way. There is no such thing as an uncoded segment with ETHNOGRAPH, however. Programs that disallow - or even discourage - researchers to browse the original context of retrieved text, are much more likely to lead them to faulty conclusions (Weitzman and Miles, 1994).

Data about data

Another way in which NUDIST and KWALITAN transcend manual methods of cutting and pasting (and therefore ETHNOGRAPH), is in their facility of adding information about the data to the data themselves. These programs are useful for adding two kinds of information to the data in particular. First, researchers can add comments about the context of data collection, speaker identifiers, or background information about the participants involved. Some of these are possible with ETHNOGRAPH's 'facesheet' facility, but with NUDIST headers are of indeterminate size. Second, researchers can summarize the content of a whole document (in profile cards or headers) or even each scene or text unit (in abstracts and subheaders). This is particularly handy for large segments because they act as a filtering system, enabling an efficient way of familiarizing researchers with the content of a particular section of data. With KWALITAN, the 'abstract' is displayed in a window adjacent to the one containing the data, both of which may be 'toggled' on and off as required. With NUDIST, these comments are written into the data files themselves, but they are distinguished from data by an asterisk that appears at their beginning and end. With every retrieved chunk of text - whether on screen or in print - the relevant 'header' and 'subheader' is also provided. Subheaders are particularly useful for data that are interview transcripts, since each question may constitute a subheader, and be printed with every text unit that is all or part of an answer to that question. Of course, subheaders and abstracts are entirely optional: they may be used at all times, sometimes, or not at all.

Lexical searching

A shortcoming of KWALITAN, shared with ETHNOGRAPH, is its incapacity to provide the automatic searching of full text - whether in data or memoranda. If researchers want to conduct even simplistic content or vocabulary analysis, KWALITAN needs to be used in conjunction with a lexical search program, such as FYI. NUDIST does provide a sophisticated a lexical search facility, however, and this is likely to be more than adequate for the needs of most types of qualitative analysis. Like FYI (and GUIDE) it includes a string search facility. But it also conducts a wide range of 'pattern based' searches via a selection of 'wildcard' characters. For example, it can search for all text units that begin with a certain word ('left anchor') which is particularly useful if subheaders are systematically used. NUDIST combines Boolean and non-Boolean operators so that text searches may be on a basis of sequence and proximity as well as context. This also extends to searches where index categories are search criteria rather than lexical items. The net effect of this facility for index searching is that NUDIST aids theory building much more than does ETHNOGRAPH's rather flat representation of relations between categories (those which do or do not both tag a segment).

NUDIST's text search is more specifically geared towards answering the types of questions inherent to theory building as opposed to general text retrieval. This is an important difference between a lexical search facility geared specifically for qualitative analysis, and a general text retriever like FYI. In particular, researchers can make the indexing system and lexical search facility interact in various ways for certain analytical purposes: in a search on a lexical item, they may restrict the search to include or exclude documents indexed at a particular node, for example. Thus, if there is one node for attendants and one for nurses, a search on 'bugs' can be restricted to each node, one at a time. By comparing the results of these searches, we may see how social rank affects the ways in which agents of contamination are perceived. Similarly, if there is a node for attendants who are at the same time sufferers of TB (such as Roth himself), the search may exclude all data indexed by this node, in the first instance, and then be restricted to only those data that had been indexed by it, in the second. Researchers may explore thereby how experiencing the disease affects the way workers perceive or translate rules concerning contamination.

The fact that headers are included in the text search is also a useful feature of NUDIST. In an interview transcript, for example, each subheader might represent a particular question, and thus is labelled 'Qu.1', 'Qu.2', etc. Here, a text search can be conducted on all occurrences of words in responses to a given question in the entire research, or indexed with a certain node, collecting all data together and saving them in one place. Furthermore, the results of a search may then be stored in a node, for example 'qi attend contam bug'. This new node may then be used as a condition for data retrieval in consequent searches. In this way, NUDIST combines lexical searching and the more conventional method of searching text via codes. In our research, this combination of strategies proved to be an invaluable tool in both the exploration of existing categories and the development of new ones.

Theory building and 'Grounded Theory'

However, there is a paradox here. Despite KWALITAN and NUDIST's greater accommodation of browsing the data, and KWALITAN's facility of retrieving lexical items in text, both programs drive analysis into the text rather less than does ETHNOGRAPH. With KWALITAN, emphasis is on writing and editing memos and, with NUDIST, emphasis is on developing and exploring an emergent index system. This, it seems, is a goal of the program's authors. These activities are vital during the early stages of analysis, but as researchers' knowledge of the data accumulates, it is elements of emerging conceptualization that produce search criteria, rather than attributes of the data themselves. This is how theory about the data develops. In the words of the authors of NUDIST, a theory building tool must go beyond browsing:

> Since the indexing system, its structure, and the changes you make to it reflect your emerging understanding, sophisticated ways of exploring it are often more important then browsing the data documents. (Richards et al., 1990a, p. 7)

and, search and retrieval:

> NUDIST can be used just to *code and retrieve text*, and it does this extraordinarily well. But it is designed to assist users who want to go further by shaping their understanding of the data and helping them to form and test their theories about the data. (Richards et al., 1990a, p. 5; emphasis in original)

For although analysis is originally grounded in the data, as the index system develops, researchers are able to move beyond the data without becoming detached from them. Analysis is thereby able to move towards the goals of grounded theory. From this perspective, this is the ultimate goal of coding and qualitative analysis - not the retrieval of text. As Richards et al. (1990a, pp. 9-10) argue:

> ... NUDIST supports "grounded theory" research (Strauss, 1987), a method that has little to do with coding and retrieval of text segments, but a lot to do with catching and interrogating meanings emergent from data. "Coding" in that method refers to a very different process from the labelling of lines of text for retrieval. Rather it is about construction and exploration of new categories *and* points of view in the data, linking these to text. (Emphasis in original)

As noted by Weitzman and Miles (1994), one characteristic of the grounded theory tradition is its inductive character. This is where first-level codes are devised, usually in the language of respondents ('in vivo' codes) which are gradually replaced by second-level or 'pattern' codes, which have more theoretical power. This process is aided by memos which apply across different data chunks, cases, or research sites. This characteristic of grounded theory makes certain demands on analysis software. These demands are at all well supported by ETHNOGRAPH but they are by KWALITAN and NUDIST. In sum, the difference between these programs is the difference between the coding of text for retrieval, and the indexing of text for theory building.

From our experience, there are two qualities in particular, shared by KWALITAN and NUDIST, which enable them to be tools for theory building. The first quality is their representation and treatment of categories, which differs considerably from more conventional coding software. For example, ETHNOGRAPH does not store or manipulate analytical categories themselves. Rather, it reads only their names or, to be more precise, where these names have been attached to data. KWALITAN, by contrast, enables researchers to attach concept cards to keywords. Similarly, NUDIST permits the storage of unlimited information about a category at a node, such as comments about the documents that belong there. Besides the definition of the category, researchers may store notes about the way it relates to others, and ideas about its development, as well as the data indexed by that node. Thus all information relevant to a given node or category are stored in the same place. In this respect, KWALITAN and NUDIST are 'knowledge-bases' as well as 'data-bases', so to speak.

This leads on to the other quality of theory building tools: if they are to be knowledge-bases, they must also be inherently flexible. Our research suggests that several conditions of flexibility can be noted here. First, there is a need for comments about categories in memos or nodes to be updated as theory develops. In this sense, both programs support the continual defining of categories essential in any kind of coding strategy. Second, researchers must be able to update how categories are attached to text. For as definitions of categories change, so do their relevance to data. With KWALITAN, the keywords for a scene may be edited at any time, and so may the indexing of text units with NUDIST. Thus, both accommodate the inductive theory building inherent to much qualitative analysis rather better than does ETHNOGRAPH.

NUDIST, however, has to contain a third level of flexibility because the index system is designed to reflect developing theory. It accommodates this rather well, however. New nodes are created as concepts emerge, and old ones may be deleted and moved as categories develop, reflecting shifts in ideas about their significance or relations to others. Indeed, NUDIST anticipates during analysis that, not only will individual nodes be created or modified, but whole clusters or 'subtrees'.

There are also other features shared by KWALITAN and NUDIST, which make them particularly effective as theory building tools. In short, they both contain 'hypertext' aspects, using the term in its most general sense. The final two sections of this chapter will introduce hypertext by looking at some of these features. The discussion will then be followed in more detail in the next chapter, which focuses on a more genuine hypertext strategy.

KWALITAN and hypertext

KWALITAN's use of abstracts and memos is unique in another respect not yet mentioned in this discussion. This is regarding how they are presented on the computer screen: rather than completely replacing the source material, they are superimposed on part of it (figure 4.4). As we shall see in the next chapter, this is rather like the pop-up windows linked to note buttons in GUIDE. This has the effect of making the distance between difference sources of information seem smaller, and the relation between these sources less abstract, as we are able to switch between them with ease.

KWALITAN has other features that are similar to hypertext programs. First, with hypertext systems, memoranda are objects in the same way as data. For example, GUIDE itself does not distinguish between them as being different types of information. Thus, researchers can create buttons in and between memoranda, and search their text for words, in the same way as with data files. The difference between these two particular programs is of course that only one is specifically for qualitative analysis: KWALITAN specifies files for data, types of memoranda, and other sources of information. Thus, analysis with this program basically consists of filling them in. But the distinction between data and memos is not absolute in this sense. With KWALITAN, researchers are able to organize and analyze memoranda in a very similar way to data.

More specifically, at some point, analysis will produce a substantial amount of information about the data - and the analysis itself - which are recorded in various types of memos. Once this point has been reached, researchers can save memo files as 'raw' documents, with separate memos

110

defined as separate scenes, and they may also attach a keyword to each scene (Peters and Wester, 1990, p. 160). Researchers are then able to approach the memoranda systematically and re-analyze their original thoughts in the same way as they would data - via browsing, and editing and searching for keywords. Alternatively, this may simply serve as a more efficient indexing of memos. The same is also easily achieved with NUDIST, since documents or memos can be saved as ASCII files, introduced into NUDIST as rawfiles, and than indexed in the same way as online data documents.

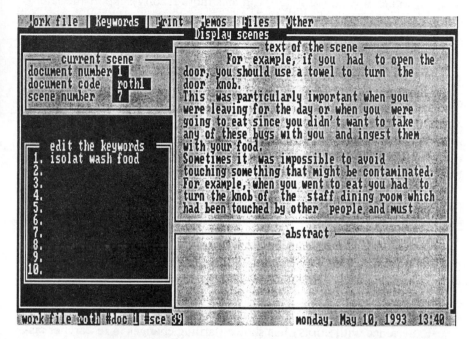

Figure 4.4 **Multiple windows in KWALITAN. Researchers can 'toggle' various windows on and off according to their requirements. This screen displays a 'scene' as it was imported into the program. As analysis proceeds, more keywords will be added in the keywords window. As the empty window implies, this particular scene does not have an abstract.**

This practice is theoretically possible with ETHNOGRAPH. However, the preparation of coded files is so much more complex and time consuming, that it is not worthwhile in most cases. It would also seem a relatively fruitless exercize in comparison, because it relies on a static representation of knowledge, and this is inappropriate for the development of theory. Thus researchers are unlikely to engage in this activity. Indeed it seems that, of the programs designed specifically for qualitative analysis in this book, there is a difference of assumption regarding the necessity of systematically re-examining or organizing analytical notes. This seems to be a requirement not only for the development of theory that fits the data, and for building new ideas upon old, but also for emerging theory to be reflexive. At any rate, the programs certainly vary in the extent that they accommodate the analytical process: although ETHNOGRAPH is an adequate tool for automatic searching, KWALITAN and NUDIST also have features that are useful for researchers to interpret and comment on the results of searches (and thus to stimulate new ones). In other words, the latter programs more readily support the later or more advanced stages of analysis.

NUDIST and hypertext

With NUDIST, relations between categories are expressed in the very structure of the index system. This is the focus of the close of this chapter, because it is the most revolutionary feature of the program. As stated by Richards et al. (1990b, p. 23), since in the index system researchers store their structural understanding of concepts and themes, '[t]he relationships these ideas have to each other ... are expressed in part by the positions they have in the index tree hierarchy'. NUDIST therefore forces researchers to think about the relations between categories more than do conventional coding and lexical searching software. Indeed, it is this aspect of NUDIST's index system that shares many characteristics with a hypertextual representation of categories. The actual structure of the index system reflects the growing structure of analysis and emergent theory. This is precisely what makes NUDIST (and GUIDE) much more than a filing cabinet or tool for organizing data: it is organization in itself.

The methodological implications of this are far-reaching - especially the way it reshapes the research process. To quote NUDIST's authors at length:

> Experience with NUDIST has shown startling changes in researcher tasks and time compared to code-and-retrieve methods, arising from the ability to construct and explore an indexing system that is an image of and container for thinking about the project. Surprisingly high proportions of time are spent exploring and interrogating the growing index system. It offers a powerful window on the state of the project, the amount of data collecting in each area under investigation, and the need for new directions of data collection. (Richards et al., 1990a, p. 9)

These implications will become clearer in the next chapter, for the hypertext strategy implies similar - but more fundamental - consequences for qualitative analysis.

5 Hypertext

Introduction

This chapter examines a relatively new genre of software, both in computing generally, and CAQDAS in particular. In short, hypertext consists of a highly flexible, interrelated database management system (Tesch, 1990, p. 288). Chunks of text are joined together in meaningful ways by electronic links, which are activated by 'soft buttons'. The latter offer the hypertext reader various pathways or trails through text. As such, text in a hypertext system is multisequential, multilinear, and multidimensional (Landow, 1992, p. 4).

Hypertext programs for qualitative analysis are increasing in number. In the late 1980s, the advent of programs such as HYPERCARD facilitated the development of complex applications by non-experts in computing (Fielding and Lee, 1991). HYPERCARD (for the Macintosh) and GUIDE (for Microsoft Windows) are both hypertext systems and programming languages. These languages are very accessible because they are 'high-level': they resemble human language. This aspect of both hypertext programs has several implications for CAQDAS. First, it enables social researchers to design programs more easily for the consumption of their peers, and this has created a wave of hypertext programs specializing in qualitative data analysis. But, more radically, HYPERCARD and GUIDE may promote diversity in CAQDAS to such an extent that each researcher has their own version of a hypertext program for qualitative analysis, tailored to their individual needs.

The representation of these developments in hypertext and qualitative analysis software in methodological discourse are beginning to gain momentum. In particular, the experiences of specific researchers with specific hypertext applications, such as HYPERRESEARCH (Hesse-Biber et al., 1989), HYPERCARD (Davies, 1991), KANT (Cordingley, 1991), and MARTIN (Walker, 1993), have been documented. Second, there is work which documents the technical aspects and structures of hypertext programs like HYPERQUAL (e.g. Tesch, 1990). Third, there are publications which take a more general philosophical or theoretical perspective of hypertext (e.g.

Landow, 1992; Bolter, 1991). All three types of literature are undoubtedly of interest to the qualitative researcher. However, those researchers who work with an IBM compatible PC will have noticed that in all these contexts there is a gap: nearly all hypertext applications for qualitative analysis are based on HYPERCARD, and thereby confined to a Macintosh environment. This chapter focuses on one program that is not: GUIDE. Although this program is not specifically designed for qualitative analysis, we argue that it can be usefully employed for this purpose. By drawing upon our experience with GUIDE, this chapter examines hypertext as a generic strategy for qualitative analysis, exploring its alternative ways of browsing, searching and organizing data (as compared with lexical searching, coding or indexing). But first it will outline the concept of hypertext in more detail.

Hypertext: the concept

Any discussion of the concept of hypertext must begin by defining the meaning of 'hyperspace'. Hyperspace depicts a geometry with many dimensions. According to psychological theory, the human mind is the ultimate exemplar of multidimensional geometry. The hyperspace of the human mind consists of associative networks. Knowledge is stored in schemata which are mental constructs for ideas. Many schemata constitute a schema: a schema represents a mini-framework in which more specific elements of information are organized into a single conceptual unit. The resulting web of interconnected concepts constitutes the semantic network. The most common conceptualization of this network is the active structural network. This consists of nodes of information or ideas which are structured by ordered, labelled relations or links: 'The nodes are token instances of concepts or propositions, and the links describe the propositional relationships between them' (Jonassen, 1990, p. 143).

Since cognition involves hyperspace, it has been argued that tools designed to aid cognition must respect this hyperspace. Computer tools for authoring novels or tutoring students, for example, must respect the hyperspace of concepts implicit in the text to facilitate reading, writing and learning. In reading, the text is absorbed by the mind of the reader, whereas, in writing, the mind of the writer is put into the text (Rada, 1991, pp. 1-3). Both involve thinking which is a complex, non-linear process. This is illustrated by Conklin (1987, p. 32):

> The thinking process does not build new ideas one at a time, starting with nothing and turning out each idea as a finished pearl. Thinking seems rather to proceed on several fronts at once, developing and rejecting ideas at different levels and on different points in parallel, each idea depending on and contributing to the others.

Thus, an ideal tool for reading and writing would respect all of these attributes of cognition. Many writers believe that, compared with other types

114

of software environments, hypertext offers the most promising computing-based medium for thinking.

Whereas 'hyperspace' refers to multidimensional space, 'hypertext' refers to multidimensional text. First developed by Vannevar Bush in 1945, the idea behind hypertext is to replicate artificially human mental processes. The aim was to provide, thereby, a system which facilitates some of the speed and flexibility characteristic of the mind following an 'associative trail' (Conklin, 1987). The structural representation of information in the hypertext database approximates the way knowledge is represented in the human mind: it is organized in terms of nodes and links. These nodes and links allow a multidimensional representation of the text and, while engaging in reading and writing the text, users may explore ideas in associative trails in much the same way as they do in human memory. This means that hypertext is more complementary to the thinking process than is the more traditional linear representation of text. In the latter, the medium of print largely restricts, squashes or flattens out the flow of reading to follow the flow of linearly arranged passages.

Furthermore, traditional text can be restricting when following side-links - an activity fundamental to any kind of research. Most textual references can be traced to their referent (target), such as a bibliographic item or footnote, fairly easily. However, often they can not be traced so easily in the other direction (Conklin, 1987); most references cannot be traced backwards from the referent to the reference unless readers can remember which path through the material they originally followed. Second, annotations must be squeezed into the margins or placed into a separate document. We cannot adjust the text in a printed book to make room for analytical notes.

Both of these inconveniences are minimized in hypertext. First, since readers may search for both referents and references with ease, since they may be linked together. and even to others in crossreferences. These links form a 'hypertext trail'. It is via such trails that paths through the text are memorized by the computer and can be reactivated. Second, the reader's notes and comments are spontaneously added to the hypertext. All text in this system is 'virtual', and thus easily changed: like in a word-processor, text simply moves along to make room for inserted writing, or closes around deleted writing. Thus, the reader's thoughts may be incorporated easily into trails, and therefore browsed and searched.

However, there are also disadvantages. Two problems with hypertext are noted by Conklin (1987). First, there is the problem of 'disorientation'. This can occur when reading or writing any kind of text, when readers are unable to find the information they require. But, whereas in a linear text readers only have the options of searching earlier or later in the text, the hypertext offers more dimensions in which they can move, hence increasing the risk of becoming 'lost in space'. Users of hypertext are likely to experience not only ambiguity in locating themselves in the hypertext, but also how to get to another place in the network. This may result in information being hard to find or even lost altogether. These negative consequences are likely to be particularly serious for hierarchical hypertext systems 'which seem to be reticent about divulging information unless the user asks the right questions in the right order by selecting the appropriate soft buttons' (Benest, 1990, p. 53).

However, disorientation in 'conceptual space' is undoubtedly beneficial to some users in certain contexts. Mayes et al. note this with regard to exploratory learning, or where the user aims to discover or create the structure underlying information. They argue:

> Since the point of discovery-learning is that the learner is continually engaged in a process of trying to map the information being discovered onto her own developing framework of understanding, then 'getting lost' may be regarded as a desirable or even necessary part of the process of structuring (Mayes et al., 1990, p. 125)

Rather, they believe that the issue which needs attention regarding hypertext is the way it enables users to create an orienting structure. Hypertext may therefore be particularly useful in qualitative research where the point of analysis is to discover pattern and connections in data. Hypertext supports analytical activities whereby researchers structure data in a meaningful way, reflecting these patterns and connections. Thus, with hypertext, the structuring of data is completely emergent from exploring them, rather than being predefined.

The second problem identified by Conklin (1987) is the 'cognitive overhead' or weight of decision-making associated with creating, naming and keeping track of links. This occurs especially when writing down ideas that are hazy and tentative. Summarizing underdeveloped ideas and knowing where to store them or what to link them to can be difficult during first stages of conceptualization. Cognitive overhead may also be experienced when simply reading a hypertext. This may be caused, for example, by the high level of concentration necessary for pursuing multiple tasks at once.

A likely scenario here is that students using a hypertext package for learning about postmodernism may want to pursue two questions at once, such as 'what are the important features of postmodernism?' and 'what are its methodological implications for empirical research?' Although these questions are related, and may even have been conceptualized while reading the same introductory paragraph in the hypertext, at some point they will lead students down diverging paths. In such cases, readers of hypertext will experience difficulty in deciding which trails to follow and which to ignore, especially when they are presented with a large number of choices. These choices require 'a certain overhead of metalevel decision making' - an overhead that is largely absent when reading linear texts (Conklin, 1987, p. 40).

Thus, even in theory, hypertext is not suited to all types of tasks relating to learning or the presentation of information. This is argued by Conklin (1987, p. 40) who concludes that:

Hypertext simply offers a sufficiently sophisticated"pencil" to begin to engage the richness, variety, and interrelatedness of creative thought. This aspect of hypertext has advantages when this richness is needed and drawbacks when it is not.

The remainder of this chapter will discuss these issues in more detail, and examine how some tasks are (and are not) suited to hypertext. In particular, it will examine whether hypertext is complementary to some of the tasks characterizing qualitative analysis.

Hypertext and qualitative data analysis

Reading, writing and thinking online

If hypertext is useful for creative reading and writing, it is potentially invaluable as a strategy for qualitative data analysis. When reading text, we are able to reveal more relevant information, whether it is more general and abstract or more specific and detailed, or associated in some other way. Material which is not relevant to our interests remains hidden. Material that is activated but then considered not relevant, can simply be folded away again, without losing our original position in the hypertext. In short, hypertext enables 'active reading', where readers construct or weave their own pathways through the text according to their interests.

Equally, the hypertext narrative, which can be 'represented as a tree diagram or flow chart', is a useful format for sociological writing: 'It's a great way to get started writing. You can put your ideas in separate boxes, rearrange them, put them inside one another, and thus gradually create a coherent whole out of a set of haphazard observations' (Becker, 1994, p. 6). In particular, Becker continues, 'writing in hypertext solves the classic problem of writers who don't know what to say first, because everything presupposes everything else'. Hypertext can solve this dilemma by leaving it to both writers and readers 'to retrieve what they need, when they need it'.

More specifically, hypertext is useful for forms of reading and writing which characterize qualitative data analysis. Here, the two activities are dialectically related: they interact with and shape each other. Researchers engage simultaneously in the reading of fieldnotes and the writing of analytical memoranda. Hypertext not only supports reading and writing individually, but also in relation to each other: it supports the interaction between reading and writing which constitutes analysis. This characteristic of analysis is described by Miles and Huberman: 'Writing, in short, does not come after analysis; it *is* analysis, happening as the writer thinks through the meaning of data in the display. Writing is thinking, not the report of thought' (1984, p. 91; emphasis in original). Furthermore, hypertext tools enable researchers to write comments on or draw out specific information from fieldnotes as they occur, and in a way that does not lose contextual meaning.

Researchers can move easily between memo and fieldnote; referent and reference.

It can be argued that one of the main reasons why hypertext is useful for reading and writing, is that the thinking inherent to these activities is largely accomplished 'online'. When using hypertext, thinking is done by interacting with text in its 'soft' form (on the computer screen) as opposed to its 'hard' form (on paper). This is partly because, although the user may print out a hypertext trail, the non-linear features (i.e. links) do not transfer to the conventional page. Thus, as noted by Cordingley (1991, p. 176), it follows that 'if the hypertext tools of today were used for analysis, the analyst would have to rely on on-line scrutiny for validation, verification, and negotiation of meanings in which links are crucial'.

Indeed, even if the representation of links in print technology could be improved, it is unlikely that browsing trails in printed hypertext would be as effective. This position is taken by Cordingley. She writes that such improvements would not necessarily overcome the Western strategies of reading from left to right and from top to bottom. This is because, unconsciously, we tend to read a 'natural order' into the information being presented, whether or not there is any implied sequencing between nodes. Thus reading strategies inherent to hypertext are less 'natural' than those inherent to other (more conventional) types of analytical technique, for example where hard-copy fieldnotes are coded chronologically. Of course, those reading strategies classified as 'natural' are not necessarily the most productive for qualitative analysis. In any case, Cordingley's (1991) observations support our argument here. It is precisely because the reader is inclined not to follow links and crossreferences that thinking in hypertext is so valuable: they can be viewed very easily. What Cordingley describes as 'natural' reading habits only apply to printed texts. If thinking is accomplished through interacting with soft rather than hard text, new reading strategies are introduced, as noted by Landow (1992, p. 4): 'Although conventional reading habits apply within each lexia, once one leaves the shadowy bounds of any text unit, new rules and new experience apply'. It needs to be considered what exactly these new rules and experiences are, and how they affect the thinking process in qualitative analysis.

It may be argued that reading and writing in electronic hypertext is more suited to the activity of thinking than is reading and writing on paper. This is because of the existence of mechanized links which facilitate a non-linear representation of the text, and because all text is 'virtual'. This may have functional consequences for the thinking process in several ways. First, it encourages a more flexible approach in memo writing - a central activity in qualitative research - because it allows an easy movement between memo and datum. This is necessary for the re-examination of data and the modification of interpretations embodied in memos as new ideas come to light. The ease of movement increases both the accuracy of the researchers' notes and comments, and their use to GUIDE other decisions and interpretations. These advantages to the thinking process are more difficult to achieve when memo writing is in 'hard' form and handwritten on the paper page or in the soft form of a word-processor file (spatially separate from analyzed data). In the latter cases, following links is much more cumbersome and time consuming, and thus the researcher is less likely to make use of linked material.

However, the downside of thinking online is that any difficulties experienced by researchers of reading from a VDU are amplified. This is in contrast to other microcomputing strategies for qualitative data analysis, as exemplified by FYI or ETHNOGRAPH, where thinking is primarily done by interacting with paper printouts. With these programs, text is searched and printed onto paper prior to detailed reading, or intermittently during the analysis process, so that thinking about data is accomplished primarily offline.

Grounded theory

Mayes et al. (1990) argue that hypertext is useful when the user's task is to discover or create the underlying structure of material. This is where there is no conceptual structure available at the beginning of the learning process in a tutorial hypertext, or desirable at the beginning of data collection and analysis in qualitative research. Thus hypertext would seem an appropriate strategy for analysis in research that adopts the idea of grounded theory - where knowledge is data-driven rather than theory-driven in the first instance. In this context, the disorientation 'risk' of hypertext translates as more of an asset than a problem. By exploring the data, researchers begin to create an orienting structure. They develop concepts with which to navigate through the data, and in turn develop theory. All of these activities are grounded in the data.

Furthermore, this process of developing an orienting structure and organizing text accordingly is an ongoing one. Even though ideas are mostly tentative in the early stages of analysis, researchers are free to explore any idea as it emerges, to create new paths, and to add to the database. This is because they can easily be modified if they prove to be inappropriate. Indeed such ideas almost inevitably will become inadequate and require modification, as analysis proceeds and ideas develop, and researchers view the same data in a new light.

This nature of qualitative research is supported by hypertext because it enables a constant comparison between the data and the researcher's ideas so that ideas are free to develop and thus maximize their validity. As Cordingley (1991, p. 172) notes, inconsistencies may be seen through a process of 'verification by inspection': through a simultaneous examination of materials, the researcher is better able to see inconsistencies and errors and to check the faithfulness of interpretations. Furthermore, the possibility of tracing one's footsteps and re-examining analytical decisions is vital for reflexive methodology, which is currently highly valued in qualitative research.

All of this means that researchers may incorporate ideas into the hypertext, no matter what their stage of development. Since these ideas may be revisited at a later time, and changed if desired, the chance of forgetting or losing information which could prove to be important is reduced. It may also help maintain a greater diversity of ideas given the tendency for researchers to become preoccupied with pursuing the ones that develop the most quickly. Thus, it would seem from this discussion of the general features of qualitative research that hypertext will be a valuable tool for researchers since the 'dynamic, associative and non-linear character of hypertext probably mimics quite well the heuristic and iterative processes typical of qualitative analysis' (Fielding and Lee, 1991, p. 117).

Data display

Hypertext seems to have advantages for the methods of 'data display' which, according to Miles and Huberman (1984), is 'an organized assembly of information that permits conclusion drawing and action taking'. These devices for reducing and organizing data have a central role in any kind of analysis. The traditionally dominant form of display in qualitative research has been the narrative text. However, as Miles and Huberman note:

> Our experience tells us that narrative text alone is an extremely weak and cumbersome form of display. It is hard on analysts, because it is *dispersed*, spread out over many pages and is hard to look at; it is *sequential* rather than simultaneous, making it difficult to look at two or three variables at once; it is usually only *vaguely ordered*; and it can get monotonous and overloading. The same objections apply with even stronger force for final readers. (Miles and Huberman, 1984, p. 79; emphasis in original)

Increasingly, other types of display have been encouraged in qualitative analysis, to include charts, diagrams, tables and matrices, which pull together strands of text.

Hypertext may facilitate efficient data display by avoiding some of these problems. First, attention may be drawn to the analytical relation between different strands of text by joining them together via a topic or variable chart, such as in figure 5.1. This is similar to the activity of recontextualization which characterizes the coding segments strategy. Except, with ETHNOGRAPH's mode of display, we cannot construct charts which contain comparative information about data: relevant data are simply pasted together in one place for further analysis. If further analysis is to consist of analytical charts, these can only be created independently in another program, or drawn up on paper. Hypertext has several advantages over these kinds of charts. Information contained in the chart is not obscured by obtrusive reference information (allowing researchers to find the relevant data manually if required). This is because charts are electronically linked to the data. Thus, researchers can move easily between the representation of data in terms of a particular theme or topic, to data in their original context in the fieldnotes. Conversely, when reading data in their original form, we can see if they are relevant to any topic charts (indicated by the presence of buttons), and spontaneously choose whether to view them or not.

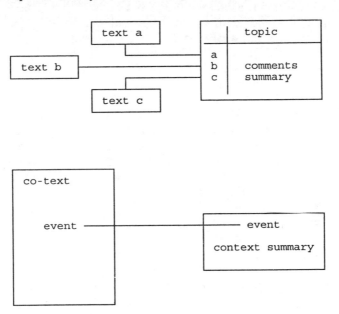

Figure 5.1 **Forms of data display. In the top diagram, individual segments of data are linked to a topic chart. This chart summarizes, compares, and comments on segments with specific reference to a particular topic. The bottom diagram shows an event context chart. An event is linked to analytical information which summarizes its context. This chart can be activated to save time reading the co-text around the segment, to find significant information.**

Hypertext is a useful tool for drawing out significant information from the data and improving analytical focus in other ways not supported by the coding strategy. For example, 'context charts', as suggested by Miles and Huberman (1984), may be added to the database and activated at relevant points to summarize important contextual information (figure 5.1). 'Variable-specific context charts' may also be used when researchers want to understand a specific variable in context, such as inter-role transactions. Context charts may be in the form of text, or relations may be depicted more graphically in the form of a diagram. For example, we could use a flow chart to illustrate informal networks among patients in the TB hospital, using arrows to indicate those patients who are most powerful, influential or popular in this context. These techniques help the analyst map individual actions into a clear context and to draw out their meaning without facing the common problem in qualitative research of being overwhelmed with detail.

Similarly, researchers may develop 'time-ordered matrices'. A central characteristic and virtue of qualitative research is that data is diachronic rather than synchronic, so that processes and sequences of events may be followed over time and analyzed. One technique of analysis is to use the temporal context of actions to make sense of them (Hammersley and Atkinson, 1983, pp. 193-4). Matrices which summarize this information are particularly useful, in that they are effective data reduction devices. As such, these charts provide a useful tool for displaying data about time-linked events to facilitate the understanding or explanation of what is happening.

All of the matrices and charts noted here, of course, are common in qualitative analysis irrespective of the computer strategy adopted (indeed, if one is adopted at all). But hypertext allows us to take data display techniques a step further: charts may be integrated directly into the database. To take the last example of time-ordered matrices, charts can draw together different events (i.e. different pieces of text) to emphasize their temporal relation without losing their original textual context (since we can move rapidly between these two representations). Second, charts and diagrams do not necessarily have to be textual, allowing them to become considerably more interesting visually and sophisticated analytically. For example, we can draw charts using a specialized drawing application, and then copy and paste them into a GUIDE document via the Windows' Clipboard.

The possibilities for using graphics and importing them directly into the hypertext are advantages unique to this strategy. The fact that charts can be drawn to a high standard easily and, most importantly, that they can be linked to data and memoranda and thus activated easily, is likely to increase their use. According to the importance attached to data display by Miles and Huberman (1984), hypertext therefore has the potential to make qualitative analysis highly effective.

GUIDE: a hypertext program

There are comprehensive descriptions and evaluations of computer programs available for qualitative analysis (for example, Tesch, 1990), in which some hypertext programs are included. However, unlike HYPERCARD - its Macintosh equivalent - there is little documentation of GUIDE, let alone information about its potential for research purposes. This section will outline, therefore, some of the basic characteristics and functions of this program, before the chapter proceeds to analyze its methodological implications for qualitative analysis.

GUIDE operates in a Windows environment. One of the most useful features of this environment, and therefore of GUIDE, is the ability to use multiple windows. We may have many open at one time, thus viewing many documents at once. By using the mouse to drag the window or its borders, they be moved or resized to suit our needs. We can move rapidly between documents by clicking the mouse onto any part of an open window, thus activating it and bringing it into focus. A second advantage of GUIDE being a Windows program is that the user can link files belonging to other Windows applications, such as WORD FOR WINDOWS and PC-PAINTBRUSH, to GUIDE documents, or import them into GUIDE as 'objects'. For example, graphics

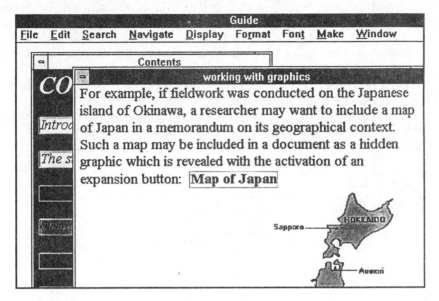

Figure 5.2 **A graphic belonging to another graphics program (PC-Paintbrush) is linked to an expansion button. It remains a hidden graphic until the button is activated.**

such as flow diagrams, maps and family trees, may be imported into a document, or linked to note, expansion, and reference buttons. Figure 5.2 shows a graphic linked to an expansion button in one of GUIDE's sample documents.

GUIDE is an object-oriented database. Files contain, and are in themselves, objects. In textual files, objects may be a word, a phrase, a paragraph, or even a whole document. One way in which a file is structured into objects with GUIDE is by inserting 'frames'. Frames provide a means of dividing a document into relatively self-contained units, sections or chapters, enabling a more efficient means of navigating through the document. But since GUIDE software also has hypermedia capabilities, objects may be modes of information other than text, such as graphics, audio or video material. These objects can be attached to note, reference, expansion and command buttons in the same way as text.

As with all hypertexts, some objects in GUIDE are 'live' in that they have behaviours as well as attributes. Such objects are called 'soft buttons'. GUIDE has four different types of buttons, each having individual attributes, behaviours and indicators: the presence of a button is indicated by the shape of the mouse pointer (or 'fly') as it passes over it. Objects can be linked together. A 'link' starts with one object (the 'source') and finishes with another (the 'target'). Buttons are generally source objects, whereas expansions, definitions, or other documents, are target objects (see figure 5.3). Since buttons are live objects, it is usually necessary to 'freeze' documents (making buttons temporarily inactive) when editing hypertexts. When editing is complete, the document must be unfrozen to make the buttons live again, enabling them to activate links. The notion of freezing the hypertext is an apt indicator of its representation of information: it is inherently dynamic.

SOURCE OBJECT	TARGET OBJECT
* reference button	* reference point in the same or a different document * another reference button * expansion button * expansion * note button * command button
* expansion button	* expansion
* expansion	* reference button * another expansion button * note button * command button
* note button	* definition
* command button	* definition

Figure 5.3 Types of objects that may be linked in GUIDE.

GUIDE has three types of buttons which may be used to structure documents: 'note buttons' display destination text in a pop-up window of a split screen; 'reference buttons' cause the window to display a different point of the document or another file altogether; and 'expansion buttons' cause previously hidden text or pictures (expanding upon the material on or around the button) to appear in the window. Button types are indicated by the shape of the mouse pointer or 'fly' when it hits a button. Each button type also has a default style: underlined text for note buttons; bold text for expansion buttons; and italicized text for reference and command buttons. (These styles can be changed by users if desired.)

Command buttons are rather different to the other types of buttons in GUIDE. Like note buttons they are linked to definitions. However, these definitions do not appear in a pop-up window when the command button is activated. Rather, definitions contain LOGiiX programming script which is then passed to interpreters in GUIDE. These interpreters allow you to do a wide range of things: open and close documents; launch other programs (even those that are non-Windows applications). For example, we may click onto a command button which takes us temporarily to a spreadsheet program, then returns to the source document in GUIDE. Furthermore, command buttons, enable users to control the serial port, activating multimedia hardware. As with note buttons, many-to-one relationships can be constructed between command buttons and definitions: a single definition can be linked to many command buttons (thus saving time invested in the repetitive writing of the same definition, as well as space in the hypertext).

Searching

Although not as sophisticated as NUDIST and FYI in its provision of searches based on Boolean operators or patterns, GUIDE has a comprehensive search facility which is useful in qualitative analysis. First, we can search for words and phrases in text. GUIDE's lexical searching facility includes several useful functions for defining the text to be retrieved and the areas of the hypertext to be searched. First, we can define precisely the required text, which may range from single characters to strings of words. This may be in either a 'simple search' (where all instances are required), or a 'complex search' (where an occurrence is only required if it appears in a certain lexical context). Complex searches use the 'and' and 'or' Boolean operators between up to four words or strings. But where precise words are less important, GUIDE also conducts searches that are more 'fuzzy' using 'wildcards' (truncated word search) and ignoring the distinction between upper and lower case characters.

A basic requirement of all database programs is for users to specify where the program should look for search criteria. But this is more complicated with hypertext. With GUIDE, users choose whether to search the active document only, the active document and those to which it is linked, or a selection of documents which then needs to be specified. Furthermore, since hypertext models of information are multilayered, the user may also specify which layers are to be searched. There are three options here: only the layers (expansions) that are presently active (i.e. where expansion buttons have been activated); all layers irrespective of whether they are active or not; and definitions (information linked to note and command buttons).

In addition to searching for words and strings in text, GUIDE provides another search facility that is exclusive to hypertext systems: we can search for specified objects and links. When these options are completed, GUIDE can 'scan' the results of the search, listing each button found alongside the text of the button. The user may then directly 'go to' a selected button, or save the search results as a 'hit list'.

Qualitative analysis with GUIDE

Note buttons

Note buttons, which use 'pop-up' windows, are a useful means of adding supplementary information to the data which may facilitate its understanding. For example, every occurrence of a person's name in fieldnotes and memoranda can be made into a note button, which is linked to background information about that person. This information is then always at hand. Stark (1990) analyzes how readers interact with supplementary information presented in the form of pop-up windows. Since pop-up windows allow a simultaneous presentation of source and supplementary information, and permit their visual comparison, it would seem that they may provide less of a memory load upon readers so that the source material is not forgotten as soon as the note is read. Also, readers may find it easier to detect inconsistencies between the source and supplementary information.

Second, pop-ups retain a constant visual context, reducing the perceived distance between source and supplementary information. Thus it follows that readers may be more willing to display information in this form than if it were presented in other ways. The simultaneous presentation of material and the smaller perceived distance between the two is important. For, as Stark notes, having 'travelled further' to see new details, readers may be 'less willing to interrupt their on-going activity' of reading to return to an examination of the source information (1990, p. 9). Perceived distance is thus vital to the hypertext principle of being able to click on to relevant information as it is required.

Thus, the note facility in hypertext encourages both the activity of adding notes to the data and referring to relevant notes whenever the data are being examined. This is because such activities are made easy and the perceived distance between datum and note is so small in hypertext. Also, the note facility encourages the reader more usefully to comprehend supplementary information since it is presented alongside the source and facilitates comparison. Though important to the analysis process, these activities are not supported by the coding segments and lexical searching strategies as represented by ETHNOGRAPH and FYI.

Reference buttons

Reference buttons and links perhaps are most usefully utilized to represent horizontal or circular relationships between chunks of information (in

126

contrast to expansion buttons which are useful for vertical and hierarchical relationships). Circular relationships are poorly represented in microcomputing strategies which organize information in a linear or hierarchical format. In hypertext, however, paths can express not only chronology or subordination (in a tree-like structure): they can also 'express cyclic relationships among topics that can never be hierarchical' (Bolter, 1991, pp. 24-5). Yet researchers will often want to link together instances in data in ways that indicate or represent horizontal or circular relationships. One event might be connected to another but not next to it chronologically in the fieldnotes. For example, in Roth's fieldnotes, reactions to a particular episode - a fight between two patients - occurred in fieldnotes days later than the event itself. All repercussions of the fight can be linked to the original episode via reference buttons. Similarly, reference links can be established between chunks of data to link all examples of a particular analytical topic or phenomenon. For example, one trail may be set up linking together those instances where violent behaviour is perceived as a manifestation of madness, and another for those in which it is constructed as direct effect of oppression or strategies of control.

Trails constructed via reference buttons can also represent particular concepts or words of interest. These can be followed and modified at any point in analysis. For example, in our research on Roth's fieldnotes, a trail for the word 'bug' was established. In the first instance, this enabled us to explore usage of the term, and the social contexts in which it appears, when interested in the constructions of disease in the TB hospital. We then linked other data into the trail where, although the word bug itself wasn't uttered, the same imagery applied. By creating the trail, we were able to ensure that our path through the data could be revisited - and indeed elaborated - as analysis progressed. More specifically, we devized different trails to represent various aspects of the word 'bug'. One trail depicted a particular usage of the word regarding its meaning (as something metaphorically evil and corrupting), and another focused on a particular context in which it occurs (while attendants are conducting their daily routines of 'isolation technique'). While following such trails, researchers are always free to browse co-text; they can abandon a trail while only part of the way through; they can move directly from the data in a trail to external information about the trail (the researcher's notes and comments about the topic); and they may construct new trails (as well as re-visit old ones) at any point in the analysis.

In addition, reference links can be used to relate other chunks of text to each other in meaningful ways. Links can be created between analytical memos focusing on various categories, pointing to horizontal or hierarchical relations between topics or themes. For example, in our research, a memo on ideas about contamination in the tuberculosis hospital contained a reference button called 'social status'. This button not only indicated an analytical link between these two categories (between ideas about contamination and the social status of those who held them), but it also enabled us to jump to the analytical memo of the related category. From this analytical perspective, researchers could then think about the relation in more detail.

Finally, reference buttons can be used to create links between the data and data display charts, a glossary of terms, or a contents list. Indeed, their uses are almost infinite: researchers may link together information from all kinds of documents, pictures, and other multimedia information with reference buttons.

Expansion buttons

Expansion buttons link vertical chunks of information. In our research, these buttons were effective devices for controlling the direction of analysis, in that we knew how to move between various levels of generality and specificity. As more information was unfolded, the greater the level of abstraction from the original text (data). At each level, we would decide whether or not to move back towards the data, or further into the realms of theorizing. For example, upon activating an expansion button in the data, GUIDE unfolds the researcher's analytical comments on the data and, in turn, reveals buttons which, if pressed, take us to relevant topical and thematic memoranda. Of course, expansion links could be used the other way round: rather than exposing more abstract notes and ideas, expansion buttons may be used to reveal information that becomes progressively more specific or detailed.

The use of expansion buttons for linking together hierarchically related information provides a useful strategy for the representation of complex relationships between analytical and theoretical constructs. Relationships between themes, topics or concepts are identified by ETHNOGRAPH in the co-occurrence of codes, and by FYI in the co-occurrence of words and phrases. In their individual ways, these two strategies indicate a possible relationship, but researchers are left to examine this relationship in analytical memoranda which are located elsewhere, separate from the data to which they refer. With hypertext applications however (and to some extent KWALITAN and NUDIST), researchers are actually able to write about the quality of the analytical relation. Their comments remain attached to data and can be easily activated. Also, the researcher may acquire more theoretical (or more specific) information, as required, by moving between the vertical levels of the hypertext (figure 5.4). Thus the situation where there is too much (or not enough) detail never arises.

This is in sharp contrast to the coding segments strategy as exemplified by ETHNOGRAPH, where all of these need to be established to some extent prior to analysis. Hypertext allows for, and encourages, far more flexibility and spontaneity in analysis. The various types of buttons and links in hypertext systems clearly have advantages for qualitative analysis. However, analysis with GUIDE also retains one of the most important aspects of the theory building programs discussed in this book. As with KWALITAN and NUDST, researchers are able to create and develop new concepts, topics and themes at any point in analysis.

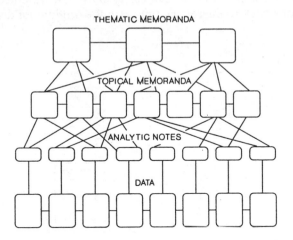

THEMATIC MEMORANDA

TOPICAL MEMORANDA

ANALYTIC NOTES

DATA

Figure 5.4 Objects and links in qualitative analysis: the structure of the hypertext

Recontextualizing data

With GUIDE, it is possible to perform analytic strategies approximating those characteristic of the coding segments strategy: data are recontextualized in terms of the topic or theme of interest to the researcher. Thus the researcher is able to reassemble all pieces of text from various places in the fieldnotes to one place so as to enhance the comparisons and contrasts which drive ethnographic analysis. However, the means by which these ends are accomplished vary between these two strategies. With the coding segments strategy, codes or tags are attached to predefined segments of text (identified by line numbers) which signify their relevance to a given category. With GUIDE, however, instead of coding the fieldnotes, researchers copy relevant segments into another document which focuses on a particular topic or theme. This may be another GUIDE document or a word processing document (requiring only minor formatting changes), both of which have several advantages over the kind of files created by ETHNOGRAPH.

One advantage of using a GUIDE file is that we can link each segment in the new file with its place in the original fieldnotes. Figure 5.5 shows an example from our research on Roth's fieldnotes. All segments relevant to the concept 'bugs' were copied and pasted into a new document or memo which focuses on this topic (figure 5.5). Each recontextualized segment was linked directly to their instance in the original fieldnotes, via reference buttons. When these links were activated, researchers could scroll through as much data around the segment as required. This means that contextual problems, often encountered when using ETHNOGRAPH, can be avoided. Only minimal and concise information need be imported into the new file because any additional contextual information can easily be found by clicking onto the button that jumps back to the relevant place in the original fieldnotes.

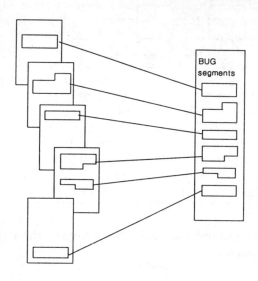

Figure 5.5 Links may be constructed between memoranda containing pasted segments and the segments in their original context in data files

It is much more cumbersome to achieve this with ETHNOGRAPH: the file name and line number, which identify the location of the segment in the original fieldnotes, would need to be noted and then entered into the search facility. Thus the process of analyzing the recontextualized data is interrupted quite severely. In order to avoid this, researchers may have to be more generous in the contextual information they include in a segment and this will result in the search file being less concise. Even then, this strategy would still prove to be inadequate for the interpretation of some passages since it is impossible to predict how much contextual information will be needed, especially when such decisions have to be made so early on in analysis (in the coding process).

GUIDE also accommodates a second way of providing the researcher with contextual information in a way that is superior to that of ETHNOGRAPH. When segments are pasted into the new GUIDE file, researchers may summarize significant contextual information and type this into the document as supplementary text. This information can then be retrieved by activating a note button when it appears in a separate window in the corner of the screen and thus supplements the data. Furthermore, GUIDE allows for the fact that what is considered to be 'significant' may vary in the course of the research process since buttons may be created, and their definitions added to and/or changed, at any point in the research.

Third, if the researchers' chosen word-processor operates in a Windows environment, they may work with this program while simultaneously analyzing data in GUIDE. This allows researchers to copy segments from GUIDE documents and paste them into another word-processing document. For example, a literature review of a particular topic had been written in the word processor, relevant examples from fieldnotes which support, expand, or contradict arguments can be pasted into the document. Conversely, excerpts from word processed documents can be imported into GUIDE documents, thus easily applying references from sociological literature to empirical data or to researchers' interpretations in analytical memoranda.

Fourth, it is possible to import whole word-processed documents into GUIDE using the 'place text' facility, and therefore create links between research papers, memoranda, and data. In contrast, with ETHNOGRAPH researchers only have the option of experimenting with the data in one program and writing and storing memoranda and research papers in the other: interaction between the two processes, via machine-supported links or by easily switching between programs and their documents, is not possible when using ETHNOGRAPH for analysis.

The ease of importing GUIDE documents into a word-processor also means that some of the inefficiencies of writing and printing with GUIDE may be overcome. Thus, when writing memoranda, the researcher may use the more sophisticated facilities for writing of the word processor and then afterwards place it in the hypertext to support further analysis. When analysis demands alterations and additions to be made to such memoranda, these can be made in GUIDE. The word processor can also be used to produce a high quality printout of memoranda and data, and thereby overcome the printing problem characteristic of hypertext tools. It is also possible to print out data complete with analytical notes which are hidden in the hypertext. Thus, the possibility of producing a hard copy of data, notes and memoranda (or indeed any object in the hypertext), means that researchers are not limited to scrutinizing them in their 'soft' form which was perceived to be one of the potential problems of hypertext tools.

Finally, the order in which segments are arranged in a search printout with ETHNOGRAPH is determined by their chronological position in the linear format of the fieldnotes. However, during analysis the researcher is likely to want to experiment with the organization of segments relating to a topic, in order to draw out similarities and differences between instances and to develop subtopics. This process is inhibited by a mere chronology of related instances. It is better supported by GUIDE's cut/copy and paste facility (and that of a word-processor) whereby researchers may easily reorganize segments to transcend the linear restrictions of fieldnotes (figure 5.6). This underlines the inherent flexibility in GUIDE, in contrast to the more rigid frameworks imposed by restricted code and retrieve procedures.

131

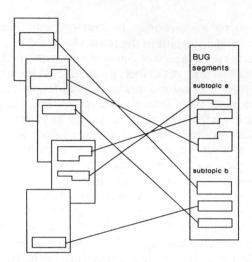

Figure 5.6 **Pasted segments may be rearranged in terms of subtopics, rather than in chronological order, and still linked back to their original context in data files**

Moving around data

With hypertext, exploring related instances in the data is not limited to the segmentation and recontextualization of text, however: the same ends can be achieved in an alternative way unique to hypertext tools. This is where links between relevant points in the text are established via the creation of 'buttons' which indicate the presence of, and are used to activate, such links. In this way, 'trails' through the data are established and these can be manipulated at any point during the analysis.

The possibility of establishing trails decentralizes the importance of moving data around and instead focuses on moving around data or, more precisely, moving between different representations of, and memoranda about, the data. What is unique about hypertext here is that, because trails may be set up so that relevant data can be easily found, segments of text do not need to be duplicated (as in figure 5.6). Rather, the content of topical memoranda may be exclusively for analytical notes in which instances are compared and contrasted, with reference buttons enabling the quick, easy return to examples in the original data file (figure 5.7).

This method is perhaps most effective for the goals of content analysis: the study of the uses, meanings and contexts of words. For example, as part of an interest in ideas about contamination in Roth's data, we were interested in the use of the word 'bug'. By using the 'find' facility, each instance where this word was used was traced by GUIDE, and researchers were then able to create reference buttons to link them. This strategy achieves similar results to FYI's lexical searching strategy. Researchers move around positions in the original fieldnotes, rather than in a file consisting of recontextualized

132

segments. Thus they do not encounter contextual problems since they are always free to browse around the word of interest at any point in the search or trail.

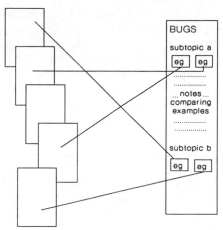

Figure 5.7 Memoranda do not need to contain 'recontextualized' segments. Data may be linked to memoranda via reference buttons.

However, what is especially useful about the hypertext trail is that, from the buttons that are present, one can see to which trails the text is related, or how a single trail intersects others. This is similar to ETHNOGRAPH's mode of data display. There, researchers can observe the codes relevant to a particular piece of text while reading through the data. Alternatively, having completed a search on a particular code, they can study the codes occurring alongside, or embedded within, or containing the code of interest. It is through such techniques, supported in different ways by ETHNOGRAPH and GUIDE, that researchers are able to begin to examine the relationships between different analytical categories, topics and themes.

However, although the hypertext trail is a useful means of connecting related instances while remaining within the same level of the hypertext (the fieldnotes), it may not be as effective when a small piece of text is relevant to a large number of different trails. For if the text is relevant to twelve categories (the maximum number of codes permitted by ETHNOGRAPH), and thus belonging to twelve separate hypertext trails, this would demand twelve separate buttons in order to retain the advantages of a hypertext strategy. Special precautions need to be taken in order to prevent so many buttons from being obtrusive to the display. Such considerations are of special importance when assessing the usefulness of hypertext, since all the thinking implicit to reading and writing during data analysis is accomplished through interacting with the information displayed on the computer screen.

In addition to being able to navigate through the fieldnotes, browsing them in their original form is a very important part of analysis. This is especially so in the early phases, since it is in these data that theory must be grounded. Thus, it is vital that computer aids to qualitative analysis support this activity. Browsing is not particularly well supported by FYI or ETHNOGRAPH. With GUIDE, however, it is easy (as long as researchers have been efficient in the establishment of links). Indeed, browsing data in their original context - as well as in terms of other analytical contexts or trails - is a central characteristic of the hypertext strategy.

In this study, links were established between data files by creating reference buttons at the beginning of each file. When activated, these took us to the beginning of the next (or last) data file. We were then able to move backwards and forwards through the days of data in a way much easier (and therefore allowing for more spontaneity in the following up of ideas) than having to open up each file individually, via GUIDE's menus. The establishment of such links between all data files also ensures that, when wanting to search fieldnotes by using the 'find' command, all data files will be searched (by selecting the 'active and linked' option, as opposed to 'active only').

The above points about moving around the data also apply to moving around memoranda about the data, or between the two: researchers may set up and explore trails in, and browse any of the nodes and links of, the hypertext at any point during analysis.

Moving between data and memoranda

Any aid to qualitative analysis should provide an easy way of moving between data in their original uncategorized form, on the one hand, and in their coded or indexed form, on the other. Accessible movement from data to memoranda is an important asset for the development of categories and theoretical constructs. For example, this guarantees quick access to already-articulated ideas, and facilitates the spontaneous writing down of new ideas as they occur to researchers while reading data.

Second, easy movement between memoranda and data provides an important methodological check in qualitative analysis: it helps to ensure that analysis is recursive, that researchers do not become too far removed from the data. Without such checks, researchers may be misled into producing distorted and artificial descriptions or explanations. This practice may also encourage new insights, and help us appreciate how data are seen in a new light as theory develops. It makes more explicit the fact that each time we look at the data, we do so with a certain idea (summarized in an analytical memorandum) in mind. Making links more explicit between data, on the one hand, and thought about data in memoranda, on the other, may help to focus the analytical attention of researchers during analysis.

Relating this requirement to the programs examined in our research, both KWALITAN and NUDIST directly support memo writing, and links between memos and data (or, more precisely, index systems) are automated, as explained in the previous chapter. GUIDE supports this practice too. However, GUIDE goes further than these programs in that links between data and memoranda are more direct: there is not necessarily an intermediate link to an index system or list of keywords. Neither does the recording or viewing of information in such memoranda have to be interrupted by reference information, since the note can be directly linked to the data to which it refers. However, since it is not a qualitative analysis program like the others, this facility is not immediately available, obvious or in-built. Instead, researchers themselves have to create bidirectional links between original data documents and recontextualized data documents, or between either of these and analytical memoranda. From there on, links can be activated with utmost accessibility and speed.

The creation of links between documents - in this case data and memoranda - is a defining characteristic of hypertext. It is also a characteristic which creates methodological implications unique to this strategy. For even though researchers may create the same links between documents as those predefined by the above theory building programs, the crucial difference is that researchers cannot take for granted which documents should be linked, or expect GUIDE to make such decisions for them. The fact that researchers have to create these links makes even more explicit the links between instances in data and abstractions or theoretical propositions. For the theoretical link is materially expressed in the hypertextual link between sentences in documents of various kinds.

The fact that hypertext allows documents to be linked together easily has other methodological repercussions, however. This is regarding, not the linking of memos to data, but rather the linking of memos to memos. For these links may encourage researchers to become so engaged with areas of the hypertext concerned with interpretation and theory that they do not often return to the original data. Thus, the advantage of hypertext for creative writing may also be seen as a possible methodological disadvantage for versions of qualitative analysis that drive analysis into the data. But for the same reason, it may be seen an advantage for the type of grounded theory advocated by Richards and Richards (1991b, p. 260), where analysis hovers over the text, then rises from it .

Data preparation and analysis as a dialectic process

With ETHNOGRAPH, coding (data preparation) is itself cumulative, dialectical, and adaptive. However, once data entry is complete (this stage has to be complete before the next stage of data analysis begins), the structural representation of data is largely static by the time real exploratory analysis begins. By contrast, there is no rigid division between data preparation and data analysis with GUIDE, in that there is no point at which one stage ends and the other begins. It may be argued that hypertext therefore provides a more flexible and dynamic approach to qualitative analysis, because

135

flexibility and dynamism are ongoing rather than being confined only to its early stages.

It is often assumed that aids to qualitative research need to have such characteristics because they are integral to ethnography. However, it is possible that too much flexibility and not enough predefined structure may leave researchers feeling stifled by the presence of too many options. 'Cognitive overload', which was identified at the outset of this chapter on hypertext, is one problem associated with lacking predefined structure. In any case, it would seem that if the text is too fluid in that it has too little fixed structure, this goes against the whole point of data analysis which, in both qualitative and quantitative research, is about imposing a conceptual structure upon (or discovering pattern within) data. Thus it seems that the ideal computer aid must get the balance right between two things. On the one hand, it must support researchers in locating pattern in data (and in structuring data in a way that makes this patterning more obvious), and facilitate thinking and writing about these patterns. On the other hand, the computing strategy must be able to accommodate the almost inevitable changes which need to be made to these structures, necessitated by a developing conceptual scheme.

There is another way in which the hypertext strategy's lack of a distinct chronological division between the stages of data preparation and data analysis may be advantageous to qualitative research. As discussed previously, the process of defining and elaborating topics is integral to data exploration and analysis. With ETHNOGRAPH, this activity is only accommodated early on in data analysis, in the coding process, after which categories become largely fixed and rigid. However, this is an activity which should not necessarily be limited to the first phase of analysis but rather be ongoing throughout the whole process of analysis. This is because, firstly, the definition and elaboration of topics cannot be adequately achieved unless it occurs alongside analysis, since the two processes are dialectically not linearly or chronologically related. Secondly, not only is the activity of defining and elaborating categories and topics necessary for the development of an organizing scheme: it is also a creative, analytical activity which triggers the asking of questions about data. Should it not therefore be allowed to occur throughout the whole process of data analysis rather than being circumscribed as a prerequisite to it?

By contrast, GUIDE does not require such a rigid structuring of activities. This is because the content of categories or topics (as represented by 'memoranda' objects in hypertext, as opposed to codes in the coding strategy) can be as fluid or as fixed as researchers desire. Thus, rather than preceding analysis, data preparation coexists with data analysis. This is because, although GUIDE has a search facility, this is more of an accessory than the fundamental tool of analysis: rather than searching for data relating to a particular hypothesis or topic, analysis takes the character of establishing new, and exploring and modernizing old, trails through the hypertext. Thus, if the main purpose of qualitative research is to gain a holistic but intricate understanding of a field which is organized by means of topics, then GUIDE is useful because it supports the development of topical memoranda as the central preoccupation of analysis. With the coding strategy however, the main part of analysis consists of starting with a system of clearly defined topics, and progresses by drawing together examples from the data which illustrate (or at most further develop) an understanding of topics and their interrelations. Thus, in a sense, it may be argued that each strategy moves in a different direction, beginning with a different premise and ending with a different objective.

With ETHNOGRAPH, we found that the linear structure of the fieldnotes necessitated an uneven development of topics. Yet this uneven development was not adequately accommodated by the coding segments strategy, which involved an analytical process which was also linear. This meant that categories which developed much later than others (because they did not become manifest until the final pages of the fieldnotes) were difficult to analyze. Since categories are relative and are defined in relation to each other, categories which emerge late in the coding process cannot be sufficiently integrated into the coding paradigm without extensive alterations to the existing system. Of course, the problems this may cause for researchers depends on the stage reached in the coding process (whether before or after the organizing system has been defined and applied to the data). However, it is likely to have wide implications, involving not only the alteration to other categories, but also the re-application of codes.

With hypertext, however, this may be resolved to some extent. Programs do not impose a linear structure on the analyst, thus allowing for the integration of any idea into the analysis no matter at what stage in the research it emerges. Indeed, the fact that topics are relative is no obstacle to hypertext since it is the relations between concepts and topics which are imperative to this analytical strategy: one of the most important tasks of the analyst using hypertext is to construct relations between such 'objects'. For example, establishing links from a memorandum on 'bugs' to other related topics, such as dirt, or more general themes, such as contamination and hygiene, is a primary occupation of the researcher: it is through navigating these links that s/he explores the data. Thus it may be argued that the hypertext strategy actually encourages the researcher to think more about the relations between categories, which are often hierarchical, as well as the binary relation between datum and category (which is the primary focus of the coding strategy). With GUIDE, physical relations (mirroring conceptual ones) between categories actually structure the way data are explored.

As argued in the second chapter, additions to the coding scheme late on in analysis also have implications for the boundaries of segments. This may be in two ways. First, in the light of a new code, all or part of a segment attributed with an old code may no longer be relevant to it. Second, re-coding the fieldnotes with a new code may mean that, on occasions, there will be too many codes for a line of text, thereby exceeding the technical limitations of ETHNOGRAPH. Both of these situations require the researcher to modify segment boundaries, but ETHNOGRAPH does not allow the researcher to do this with ease. Indeed, the only change within a coding scheme that this program does support is a change in the name of a code, as this does not involve the modification of either the content (definition) of a category, or the text to which it is relevant.

A direct comparison of GUIDE and ETHNOGRAPH is not strictly possible. This is because of the inherent differences in the structure of these programs, and in particular because of the many ways in which GUIDE can be used to structure analysis. However, it seems that hypertext does not generally entail as many problems in respect of late emerging topics. This is because links are activated by 'buttons', a specific point in the text, around which there are no boundaries as such defining the relevance of surrounding text. Thus, if a new topic develops late in the research, since links are between points in the text rather then segments, there are no boundaries to require modification. At most, buttons may need moving to a different location, or links between objects may need to be eradicated, both of which can easily be achieved with GUIDE. Furthermore, it seems that one cannot have too many links between objects, such as a segment of data, with GUIDE. In this sense, GUIDE is like NUDIST: both are the only indexing programs examined in this book that do not place a limit on the number of categories that can be applied to a text segment. Our research suggests that this is an important asset, since we often found ourselves wanting to apply more codes per line of text than is permitted by ETHNOGRAPH. However, the fact that no limit is placed on the number of soft buttons and links in the hypertext is likely to encourage a complicated network of links. In such cases, it may be difficult for researchers to be certain about which links lead from what buttons. As argued in the next section, this can be a problem in itself.

Forgetting categories and links

When using the coding strategy, we found that it was difficult to keep all codes in mind while coding the data. We tended to concentrate on categories either because their relevance was immediately obvious, or because they were foremost in our minds (they had just been applied to a previous section of data). This meant that categories that were more subtly relevant, or more distant in researchers' memory, were largely forgotten during the coding process. These categories therefore received inadequate consideration in data analysis, and thus were inadequately represented in research results. A similar problem may be encountered with hypertext strategies. Although a research project might not have a large set of 'codes' as such, it is complex in other respects. The hypertext in our research consisted of a complicated set of objects, ranging from the data themselves to analytical memoranda about the data. The latter are hierarchically related in terms of specificity and generality, with many items at each level. Unlike the coding strategy, analysis proceeds by establishing and exploring links rather than coding data and then retrieving coded segments. This, however, leaves open two levels at which problems of forgetting may occur.

First, if there are a large number of analytical categories, it may be difficult to remember every category when establishing links from data to memoranda. This has the same effect as forgetting about certain codes when coding data, thus resulting in the same problems encountered with the coding segments strategy: researchers can only explore those data and categories which can be accessed via links which they have established. Thus, when such forgetting results in the failure to establish links between relevant objects, data are likely to be insufficiently categorized, and conceptual relations between categories inadequately developed, resulting in analytical avenues becoming blocked and theoretical coherence being impeded.

However, having a large number of categories may also result in another problem which is more exclusively a risk of the hypertext strategy. With hypertext, the stage of data analysis itself consists of exploring links. Thus the situation may occur where researchers are unaware of all the objects leading from one particular button or location in the data. In this sense, there is much more decision-making involved in data analysis with hypertext than there is with the coding segments strategy. With the latter, the researcher simply chooses which codes to retrieve and the actual process of retrieval is achieved automatically by the program. However, with hypertext, at every conjunction, researchers have to decide which paths to follow. Although this may have the advantage of allowing more spontaneity in analysis, it may also result in researchers losing track of their original purpose or destination. Conversely, they may be hindered in reaching their destination due to a lack of clarity as to where each link leads, or what links must be pursued en route.

These two problems of disorientation and being 'lost in hyperspace' were identified as possible disadvantages of hypertext at the outset of our research. (In principle, these mirror phenomena associated with human memory when the mind becomes distracted and passages become blocked.) However, in context of the problem of forgetting categories, these pitfalls are amplified. First, even when researchers know what they want to find, but not how to get it (they have lost track of the links structuring the hypertext), GUIDE cannot (ironically) guide researchers here. The only option available to them here is to follow links on a 'hit and miss' basis. The difficulty in finding certain categories is thus likely to increase the frequency of the times they are neglected. This is compounded by the fact that researchers can readily follow up other ideas which distract them from this difficulty, thus abandoning and forgetting the original quest.

However, there are ways in which some of the problems above may be controlled. First, researchers may adopt a strategy similar to that of 'axial coding' where data are approached by concentrating on one topic or theme (as opposed to one code) at a time, when creating links between memos, and between memos and data. This entails approaching and interpreting the text as many times as there are categories. Or, alternatively, researchers may take a section of text and analyze it in terms of all categories, thus ensuring that all topics are considered when establishing links to and from that particular section. These two options represent two oppositional approaches to data analysis: whereas the former primarily concentrates on the topic or category, so that the whole span of the text is interpreted in its terms, the latter primarily focuses on the text (figure 5.8).

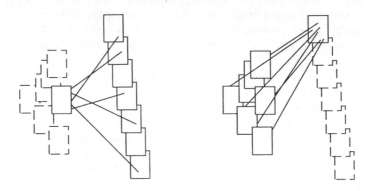

Figure 5.8 Two approaches to coding. The one on the left focuses primarily on an analytical category, whereas the one on the right focuses primarily on a segment of data.

So which coding strategy is most suited to the grounded theory approach to qualitative analysis? It may be argued, since both strategies have advantages, that they may be used conjunctively to fulfil two separate aspects of qualitative research. More specifically, the strategy which focuses on the data is a useful means of increasing researchers' familiarity with the data, and compiling a broad spectrum of topics. This facilitates a more holistic approach when the real analysis begins. By contrast, the strategy that concentrates on analytical categories approaches the data in a more selective way. This approach may therefore be more useful in a later stage of analysis: for sharpening the analytical focus of topics and theoretical constructs.

There are also ways of organizing the hypertext which can reduce the problems of disorientation and getting lost in hyperspace. First, if buttons are systematically named, GUIDE can conduct a search for a required button. This is a sophisticated facility, and one which proves to be invaluable in qualitative analysis. For example, say we wanted to retrieve background information about a certain character, such as Jimmie Shaw. We don't know exactly where this is stored. However, because of the way we decided to use the various buttons in GUIDE, we do know that it will be in a definition to a note button, and that the text of the relevant button will be 'Shaw'. Using the facility of finding objects and links, we can then specify this information, and tell the program to search the whole hypertext. As a result, GUIDE provides a list of the occurrences of these note buttons (all of which are linked to the same definition), and we can then choose one to 'go to'. This facility is only useful, however, to well organized researchers, who are aware of its possibilities and the dangers of becoming lost without it.

A second measure against disorientation is for researchers to keep a diagrammatic record or map of their progress regarding the creation of links. A map of thematic and topic memoranda, for example, may be written and stored manually (external to the database), or integrated into the hypertext as something like a contents page. Such a map should help researchers keep track of their location within the hypertext and GUIDE them around its structure, thus to some extent preventing disorientation. It may also help researchers to consider all analytical categories, and thereby facilitate their maximum development.

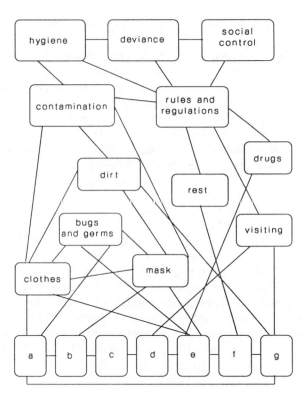

Figure 5.9 Part of a hypertextual map, showing the physical and conceptual relations between categories.

In addition, this map can be mechanized (consisting of buttons and links) so that it acts like a contents page, serving as a means of quick and direct access to the place of interest in the hypertext. A good idea is to keep the map in a place where it always accessible. In our research, the contents page was a 'background document'. This meant that part of it was always visible, and therefore could be clicked on with the mouse and activated at any time. Furthermore, each item on the contents page was a reference button, which took us to the relevant place in the hypertext. Thus, not only is the contents page very useful in that we always know where an object is, but also because it can take us directly to it. Besides being a technical tool, the map would also be conceptually useful: it could act as a 'conceptual map', indicating the various topics and themes that are conceptually linked (following the principle that the hypertext structure mimics the hyperspace of human memory and cognition). For example, a portion of our hypertextual map, which is shown in figure 5.9, shows the conceptual relationships between several topics and themes in Roth's fieldnotes.

Codes and memoranda: the representation of categories

When adopting the coding segments strategy, it soon became apparent that codes acted as key-words or prompts, or short-hand tools for representing the meaning of data in human memory. From a single conjunction of codes, researchers, equipped with knowledge about the data that had accumulated during the coding process, were able to remember a string of relevant instances in the data, most of which would have been retrieved in a search by ETHNOGRAPH. Does the hypertext strategy provide the same or an equivalent means of data reduction? Codes are the language of the coding strategy, but what is the language of the hypertext strategy? It seems that analytical categories are the terms in which one becomes familiar with the data using either strategy. But there is an essential difference in the ways these categories are represented in the two approaches. Codes represent categories which are relatively static and developed early on in analysis, and codes themselves are short-hand devices for remembering the content of these categories. Categories in the hypertext, however, which are represented by memoranda, are much more dynamic and flexible and, since access to these is easy, short-hand or summary information is not necessary. In any case, the text of soft buttons (which activate category memoranda) act as cues, but the difference is that there is no limit on the amount of text that can be included in a soft button. Furthermore, it is not a prerequisite for each button leading to the same memorandum to have exactly the same text. This is because links are electronic and prespecified.

General and specific categories

When using the programs to explore categories in our research on Roth's data, we noticed a difference in the information that was approached for analysis. For example, say we wanted to explore a general, thematic category such as social control. If using ETHNOGRAPH, a search for this code retrieves all the data that is relevant to it, including those data relevant to all its specific aspects or dimensions (each of which have an individual code of their own). Thus, in principle, general codes such as social control will be attached to a lot of data, and codes focusing on a particular aspect of social control, such as gossip, will be relevant to much less. However, our implementation of the hypertext strategy had implications for the character of this relation between thematic and general categories.

In the hypertext, the memorandum on social control was not directly linked to the data. Rather, it was hierarchically linked to other memoranda which are like subcategories, such as 'informal strategies of social control'. These, in turn, were linked to sub-subcategories, such as 'gossip'. Finally, when analytical specificity was exhausted, memoranda were linked to the data. If this method of organizing levels of the hypertext is adopted, it is only by travelling down through the hierarchy of memoranda that researchers are able to see the data relevant to a theme. Thus researchers may view the data only in terms of the specific dimensions of a theme, not in terms of the theme in general. Conversely, researchers cannot move directly from data to the thematic memoranda to which they relate, but must first travel through the intermediate levels of the hypertext.

Compared with conventional CAQDAS coding approaches, hypertext provides a much more useful means of integrating both general and specific categories into analysis. With the coding segments strategy, there is much unnecessary duplication since much data are attached to both specific topic and more general thematic codes. Also, it is rarely useful to see the data related to a very general code, since a search would retrieve too much information, and the relation of data to the theme will often seem tenuous or unclear. It is much more useful to be able to view the data in terms of the more specific aspects of the theme so one can see exactly how the data relate to it.

Lexical searching with GUIDE

Not only can hypertext accommodate to some extent the analytical principles of the coding strategy (by cutting and pasting the fieldnotes according to their relevance to analytic categories), it can also accommodate lexical searching strategies. Lexical searching is often used to pursue the goals of content analysis where researchers are interested in identifying the symbolic meaning of messages, by making explicit the context in which they occur. For this type of analysis, researchers must easily be able to search the data for specific words or strings. Programs must also help researchers to represent the results of searches in a systematic way, so that comprehension may be enhanced, patterns and relations may be constructed, and results may be related to those obtained by other methods.

GUIDE allows researchers to search for words and strings in the data using the 'and' and 'or' Boolean operators. (Indeed, researchers may search for words and strings in analytical notes and memoranda as well as in the data.) It also allows researchers to represent the results of a search in a number of ways, facilitating a wide range of approaches to lexical analysis. First, a trail which links these words together may be established. Researchers can then move through the fieldnotes by jumping from one usage of the term to another (see earlier section on 'moving around data'). Second, researchers may copy the co-text in each instance the word appears into another document dedicated to that particular phenomenon. For example, if interested in the word 'bug', a separate document may be allocated for each aspect of its usage (i.e. who uses it, in what conditions, its various meanings), and the relevant text pasted in (see earlier section on 'moving data around'). These may then be linked to a memorandum on bugs which draws together the analytical notes. Analytical notes, in turn, may be linked to a more general memorandum on contamination, and so on.

Alternatively, researchers may insert analytical information specific to each instance into the fieldnotes as they are retrieved by GUIDE's 'find' facility. Notes can be inserted in the data by creating an expansion button, and then writing them into the expansion. In future situations, this information will only be revealed if it is specifically required (i.e. the expansion button is activated). Conversely, researchers might want to summarize each context in which the word appears. They can do this by creating reference links from words of interest to a context chart, which is located somewhere else in the hypertext. This chart may be part of a memorandum on the word of interest, comparing instances in which the word is used in the data. Such memoranda facilitate the comparison of contexts, so that researchers may discover context-dependent meanings, or contextual classification, where it is expected that symbols have more in common the more alike the situation in which they occur.

Finally, hypertext is useful for a particular method of data representation common to content analysis: 'clustering'. This is where interrelated concepts are organized so that their relations in the network reflect their relations in reality. The semantic network, with its nodes and links, is an important tool of data representation in content analysis and, since the structure of hypertext systems is designed to represent a semantic network, it should provide the ideal tool for clustering. Hypertext also facilitates another condition of content analysis: to relate the results of content analysis to other methods of data analysis. Memoranda belonging to other methods (written in a word-processor) may be placed into the GUIDE, and linked to those in the hypertext. In this way, another level of analysis (and level of the hypertext) may be built, which is concerned with comparing and contrasting the results of other methods.

However, the facility that hypertext does lack is a vocabulary breakdown. As found with FYI, a vocabulary list is a useful starting point for any type of analysis, but is especially useful for any type of content analysis. This is because it is a vital tool for the construction of thesauri which are essential to any type of lexical searching strategy. Thus researchers are unable systematically to construct a list of synonyms and related terms and then search for their presence in the data. Similarly, there is no sophisticated frequency list. In other words, decisions about what is searched for with GUIDE are much more ad hoc: they are likely to be based on a qualitative familiarity with the meaning of data, rather than on knowledge about the range and frequency of words. This, of course, is not necessarily a drawback of hypertext. There is no reason why researchers cannot use the vocabulary and frequency lists provided by FYI if they want to examine the range and frequency of words as a starting point of analysis, and then analyze the words of interest as part of a more general hypertext strategy. Furthermore, for those who are interested in programming, GUIDE (and HYPERCARD) provide researchers with the means for developing such facilities for themselves.

A more qualitative strategy?

When coding the text ready for ETHNOGRAPH in our research, we often observed a direct relation between categories in the data. For example, several segments displayed a relation between flexibility and community, on the one hand, and the division of labour, on the other. More specifically, the division of labour between departments was associated with flexibility and community, whereas the division of labour between departments was associated with competition and inflexibility. However, since the principle of analysis with ETHNOGRAPH works on whether a certain code (variable, concept, topic) or conjunction of codes is present or absent in the data, it is only in these terms that a relationship between categories can be expressed. Thus, analysis using the search and retrieval procedures of ETHNOGRAPH essentially works on a quantitative principle - the distribution of codes - the results of which are qualitatively analyzed by the researcher. Thus there is no room in the coding strategy for the researcher to integrate a more explicit qualitative understanding of relations between codes into the coding process, or into the representation of data as utilized by ETHNOGRAPH. Such observations can only be articulated and built upon separately from the data in analytic memoranda.

By contrast, the hypertext strategy not only supports the explicit exploration of the relations between topics, but it also enables researchers to build observations about these into the database. Indeed, if certain relations prove to be of significance, researchers can make a relation between categories a topic in itself, allocating to it a specific memorandum, and linking this memorandum to both the other categories and the data to which it is relevant. (This can also be achieved with NUDIST, since an emergent relation between categories can itself be made into a category or node.)

Second, the fact that hypertext focuses on the relationships between topics or objects in a database enables a more holistic approach to qualitative data analysis. The relations between different phenomena are embedded in the very structure of the hypertext in terms of its links and nodes. This focus on the relations between topics enables researchers to transcend the boundaries of topics or their specific aspects, both horizontally (the researcher can see their relation to other aspects of the same phenomenon, and to other topics), and vertically (to more specific or more general topics and themes). This is in contrast with the approach encouraged by ETHNOGRAPH. With the latter strategy, it is more tempting to focus on variables depicting limited aspects of phenomena which have some rigidity - and to focus on the distribution of these variables in the data - rather than their conceptual relations. This difference reflects the fact that the hypertext strategy requires less prior conceptualization than does the coding strategy. Thus, with its need for prior conceptualization and its use of variables, it would seem that the coding segments strategy makes demands on researchers that are more characteristic of quantitative research. In these respects, the hypertext strategy is more in line with the goals and merits of qualitative analysis.

From our experience with GUIDE, the hypertext strategy encourages researchers to think more about the relations between categories. Thus it is a greater aid to both theory building and thick contextual description. Also, in contrast to the coding strategy, it supports an intimate, tight relation between data and conceptualization throughout the whole span of data analysis. This more comfortably accommodates the process aspect of grounded theory. Hypertext does not inhibit the dialectic which characterizes this relationship: it allows for changes in conceptualization, as categories and the relations between them develop and data are represented in a new light. Thus the hypertext strategy is better equipped to fulfil the principles laid down by the grounded theory approach to qualitative research. However, hypertext does introduce new techniques of reading, writing and organizing information, and thus qualitative analysis adopting this strategy involves rather new types of decision-making. The next section explores some of them.

Decision-making in hypertext

Hypertext may be conceived as consisting of different layers or segments which are both vertically and horizontally related. In our implementation of hypertext, the bottom-most layer consisted of fieldnotes. At this level, the fieldnotes appear in their original form and structure, with the exception of occasional changes in font. These changes of font signify the points at which the researcher may move onto the next layer. They also signify the type of link that will be activated. More specifically, underlined font indicated the presence of a note button which, when activated displays information in a pop up window (figure 5.10), and bold font indicated the presence of an expansion button. If the mouse pointer is moved over the bold text and clicked, the analytical note which is relevant to the segment will be revealed. The whole segment was made into an expansion button, because it was all relevant to the expanded text.

Thus, while browsing fieldnotes and analytical commentary, researchers are continually confronted with text that is underlined (note buttons), in bold (expansion buttons) or italicized (reference buttons). In such cases, they are faced with two options. First, they may treat the text the same as the rest, thereby suppressing analytical detail considered to be irrelevant to the task at hand. With expansions, the screen will remain as in figure 5.11.

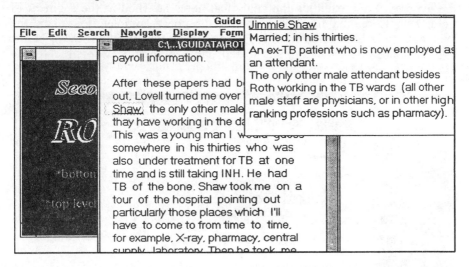

Figure 5.10 An example of the use of note buttons. When the note button (shown in underlined text) is activated, the 'definitions window' appears in the top right hand corner of the screen. The window stays open until the mouse button is released. A single definition may be linked to many relevant note buttons.

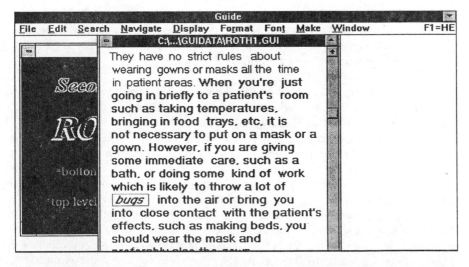

Figure 5.11 Bold text is used to indicate the presence of an expansion button. By clicking the mouse onto any bold character, analytical notes (margin comments) expanding on the data segment will be revealed.

Alternatively, we can activate the button (thereby moving to the next level of the hypertext) and examine the analytical notes attached to the segment of fieldnotes. Here, the fieldnotes do not disappear completely: rather, the analytical note is inserted into the fieldnotes so that the two layers of the hypertext are coexistent on the screen and are equally accessible to the reader (figure 5.12).

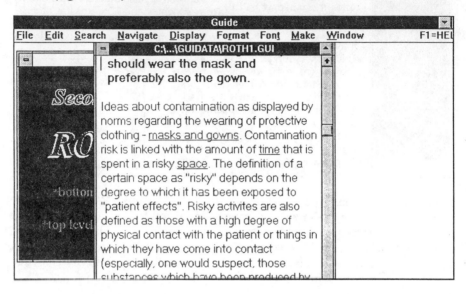

Figure 5.12 Analytical notes are activated by an expansion button in fieldnotes. The researcher is able to make a clear distinction between the two levels of information through the systematic use of colour.

However, if the latter option is taken, we are faced with yet another decision. This is because, when an expansion button in the fieldnotes is manipulated, not only are analytical notes relevant to a specific passage revealed, but also other analytical information (figure 5.13). This information is not explicit: rather, it appears in the form of a sign. The words at the end, in italics, are reference buttons, and the text of these buttons indicates the analytical categories to which the segment is relevant. In other words, rather than serving the purely mechanical function of activating a link, like codes they act as prompts, summarizing classification information. Upon reading these words, one is able to approximate how the segment fits in with other topics in the analysis. Researchers now have to decide between two options: to return to the fieldnotes (thus folding away the expansion), and back to the original task; or to proceed to a different layer of the hypertext (accessible through the expansion), such as topical memoranda.

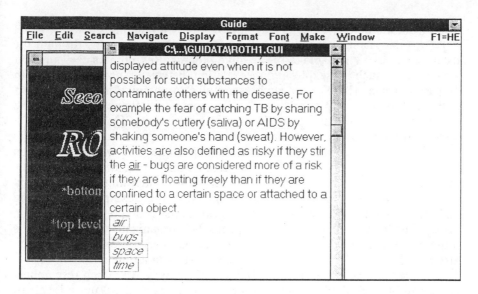

Figure 5.13 Expansions can also be linked to buttons. Thus, reference buttons (activating relevant topical memoranda) may be embedded in analytical notes.

The decision whether or not to activate a button is perhaps more important regarding reference than expansion links. This is because when an expansion button is activated, the fieldnotes automatically follow the unfolded material and thus the analytical process is interrupted only temporarily. By contrast, the text containing a reference button is completely replaced by the information at the destination of the button: the user jumps to a completely different location in the hypertext. This means that there is a greater risk of researchers becoming side-tracked with reference buttons. For example, say we were interested in the instances where masks and gowns are used in the hospital. By reading unfolded material, researchers can see that there are many meanings of contamination. We might then decide to focus on just one, such as how certain spaces come to be defined as 'dirty'. Accordingly, we can then activate the reference button labelled 'space', which takes us to a memorandum focusing on the conceptualization and regulation of space.

This memorandum, however, is linked to many others. For example, it is linked to one that contains all segments of data relevant to the regulation of space. It is also linked to a document that consists of comparative information about various instances in the data. Rather than containing pasted segments of data alongside these analytical notes, this memo has reference links which can take us back to examples in the data. Also, there are the memoranda of separate but related analytical categories such as 'bugs', 'contamination', and at a higher level of generality, 'hygiene', 'social control', and 'deviance'. Clicking onto one of these takes researchers further again from the fieldnotes. This may have one of two outcomes.

First, granting researchers such flexibility in choosing paths through the database is more amenable to the creative process. Researchers can pursue a single task (such as exploring the relation between space and dirt) in numerous ways. Thereby, researchers are able to perceive the phenomenon in the light of many topics and themes. This may facilitate new ideas, and the establishment of new nodes and links to represent them. On the other hand, movement between segments and layers of the hypertext may progressively side-track analytical attention. Rather than pursuing the original question (how do certain spaces come to be labelled as dirty?) we might change our question and path through the data in search of something quite different (what rules are most commonly broken?). This is because problem-solving and task formation with hypertext largely takes the character of following a 'stream of consciousness', so to speak. No organizational structure is imposed on analytical activity. Such distractions may be creative, but may also result in some ideas not receiving the development they deserve.

This section has hitherto explored some of the ways in which researchers can move through the hypertext from the bottom level (data) up to levels of theorizing (analytical notes and memos), which become increasingly general and abstract. It may be argued that this encourages an inductive approach to analysis and theory building. However, with hypertext it is also possible to move in the opposite direction: from top to bottom. Researchers may select a particular proposition or component of a theory, and then work downwards (through analytical categories and finally to data) to test or explore them. Thus hypertext also enables researchers to take a more deductive approach.

Indeed, the way that we used hypertext in our research made it possible to begin a path at any point in the hypertext, and to work in any direction from it. This is because our title page, which opens as soon as we start up the hypertext on Roth's data, is essentially a contents page. This document stays in the background of the screen (as can be seen in most diagrams in this section), and thus can be activated at any time. It is like a contents page because it is linked to two other documents that separately list data and memoranda. These documents are hierarchical: by using expansion buttons to unfold detail, links to all the nodes in the database, ranging from the individual data files to the most abstract of themes, are revealed (figure 5.14). The flexibility a contents page enables is an asset to analysis and accommodates individual differences or personal style. The way the hypertext is structured is entirely in the control of the individual so the eventual structure should reflect the individual's style of analysis.

This leads us to a very important point about hypertext. The eventual structure of a hypertext not only says much about the researchers' style of analysis, but also provides invaluable insights into how they have reached their conclusions. For this reason, hypertext is a very useful tool in secondary analysis. For example, say Roth had originally used a hypertext when analyzing his data, and that he had made this available to other researchers. By navigating through his hypertext, we would be able to see how he had organized and classified his fieldnotes, and the paths he had constructed through the data and his analytical notes and memos. In other words, we would have been able to trace the decisions that led Roth to his conclusions. This way is much more insightful than if we were to examine his fieldnotes, analytical notes, and working papers in their disparate and handwritten or printed form.

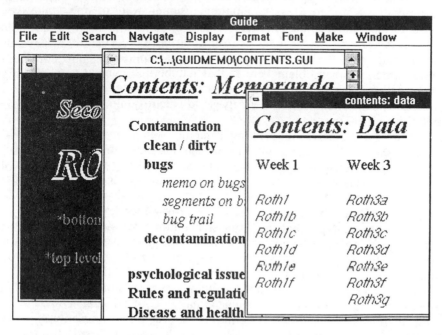

Figure 5.14 By clicking onto a topic, subtopics are revealed and, in turn, so are individual files relating to each subtopic. The latter, appearing in italics, are reference buttons which, when activated, take the researcher directly to the file of interest.

Another issue is relevant here. Although secondary analysis using the other two programs is likely to encourage different results, GUIDE is much more likely to render the analysis a highly personalized process. This is because GUIDE does not structure analysis, but rather provides researchers with the tools to structure it for themselves. Thus, different researchers will reach highly differing interpretations of the same data. The question that arises here, however, is the extent to which the results of research using GUIDE is method-dependent. For the method upon which the results depend is not so much the mode of data collection (ethnography) or the instrument of analysis (hypertext) but rather the specific way GUIDE is used for analysis.

The previous section examined some of the decision-making processes characteristic of analysis with a hypertext program. This section discusses the extent to which directional decisions, which carve particular pathways through the hypertext, are reflected in a printout. This topic raises itself as an issue because the concept of hypertext is at odds with the idea of printing: the product of hypertext is a multidimensional web of interconnected information, whereas the product of printing is a linear document. Furthermore, the principal means of selecting the parts of a document for printing with GUIDE (like most word-processor programs) is by selecting page numbers. The problem here is that numbers are linearly related so, although they are perfectly adequate devices for ordering a linear document, they do not easily lend themselves to identifying a path through multidimensional text.

This has consequences for printing different types of trails with GUIDE. On the one hand, GUIDE is adequate for representing a trail in printed form if it simply involves examining one document (such as a day of fieldnotes) in a chronological manner, and revealing other layers of the text (analytical notes) here and there. In other words, GUIDE may easily print a trail that involves expansion buttons, and thus may print either figures 5.10 or 5.11 above with ease, depending on expansion buttons remain activated at the point of printing. (We can also command GUIDE to print all layers of a document, irrespective of whether they are active or not.) Printing information contained in note definitions is less straightforward, however. This is because as soon as the mouse button is released note buttons cease to be activated: definitions are not visible at the point of printing. The outcome of this nature of note buttons, if definitions are required in a printout, is that they will appear at the end of the document, instead of beside the text to which they are relevant. This is a limitation which needs to be considered when note buttons are created and their purpose is conceived.

Of course, trails do not simply involve moving between the different layers of a document (via expansions and note buttons). Indeed, trails primarily involve moving between different documents, or between different parts of one or more documents, via reference buttons. Thus an important question here relates to how these movements are represented in printed material. For example, if we began our path by engaging on a pre-established 'bug' trail (jumping between each instance of the word in the data), unfolding relevant analytical notes as we go, and on occasions moving to relevant memoranda, how might our progress be recorded in a printout? Can a pathway through multidimensional text, such as that in figure 5.15, be represented in a linear printed document? It certainly is not straightforward.

Ideally, all material that had been uncovered could be printed, like the results of a search with FYI or ETHNOGRAPH. But this cannot be achieved with hypertext. This is because, in order to print with GUIDE, page numbers have to be specified. In short, it seems that inter-document trails, or those that jump between separate points within the same document, largely can only be represented or examined in soft form.

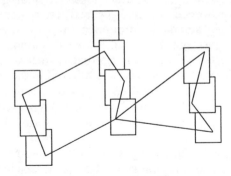

Figure 5.15 A trail through hypertext documents via reference links

Indeed, the only way it seems possible to record such a trail would be to copy and paste each of its constituent parts into a new document. (This process is similar to the recontextualization of segments characteristic of the coding strategy, except that it is not only the fieldnotes that are involved in this process but also reflective thoughts on the fieldnotes and topic of study.) Thus, this new document represents a specific trail through the hypertext and, since in itself it is a linear document with page numbers, part or all of the trail can be easily printed.

The ability to print with ease is important because there is a limit to how much exploring one can do in soft form before it is necessary for some hard copy feedback that is both tangible and permanent. Also, printed trails are an important aspect of the writing-up stage of ethnography or any qualitative research, as each trail represents how an idea was followed through. But the problems attached to printing in hypertext becomes less of a problem if hypertext is allowed to influence modes of dissemination in ways that are quite profound, as we will see in the next section.

Writing up

Finally, there is another way in which hypertext may be a useful tool in qualitative research. Unlike facilities in other microcomputing strategies discussed in this book, this possibility fundamentally challenges the conventions of ethnographic writing. Although there is not the space to examine this possibility in depth here, as the focus specifically is on data analysis, it seems that hypertext has the potential to revolutionize the way that research results are presented and disseminated. Hypertext challenges the form of the final stage of qualitative research - the ethnographic monograph - itself.

The usual structure of the research process is that data analysis (via conventional manual methods or computer aids) produces analytical notes and memoranda. Those points considered to be significant, interesting, or substantiated are extracted from these products of analysis, and then reassembled and padded out to construct research findings. Findings are written up in a word-processor and printed as a conventional linear document, which is then amenable to publication as a book or monograph. Although this usual passage may be followed having used hypertext programs such as GUIDE for analysis, alternative means of disseminating results may be considered. Results may be published in the form of hypertext so that results are sold or distributed on floppy disk rather than as a book. For example, Roy Rada's (1991) book, entitled 'Hypertext: From Text to Expertext', is also available for purchase in the form of hypertext on a floppy disk.

So what are the possible advantages of this? For some time now it has been noted that hypertext programs are useful in teaching. An obvious advantage, for example, is that it may cater for individual differences in learning ability or interests: individuals may suppress or reveal layers of detail to fit their requirements. More aesthetically, with their soft buttons, colourful fonts and graphics, multiple windows, and hypermedia possibilities, programs such as GUIDE perhaps offer a more exciting and interactive mode of learning than the printed textbook. But are there similar advantages in producing hypertexts for authors who are qualitative researchers, or readers who are interested in qualitative research?

Regarding the first question, if a hypertext strategy of data analysis is adopted, researchers will have already accomplished much of the work involved in writing a hypertextual monograph. Since the data, and all products of analysis, exhibit a hypertext structure, we are much closer to achieving our ethnography in hypertext than in linear form: writing-up is largely a matter of carefully editing the database. In fact, having to move from hypertextual to linear forms of representing knowledge is likely to introduce far more problems into the writing up stage of research. As for the second question, the reader of an ethnographic (hyper)text is easily able to follow crossreferencing: this involves a click of the mouse rather than manually having to find the right page number and part of the page.

Referencing is an important aspect of any academic project. In the first place, there may be referencing in the form of footnotes. In the hypertext, these references can be represented by buttons which take us to specific authors or texts in a bibliography. More specific to empirical research, there may be automatic links to data and appendices. In the second place, there is a crossreferencing of topics in most academic work. This is especially the case in ethnographic writing. These texts are likely to comprize of a high number of interrelated topics, because they are based on a holistic conception of research, which attempts to grasp a large variety of interrelated phenomena. Again, the hypertext mode of dissemination is an ideal way of representing this kind of work.

With all these types of referencing and crossreferencing which characterize ethnographic writing (and indeed, other types of empirical research), the link between referent and reference can be automated using note and reference buttons in a hypertext. This makes the reader's task of following references much less time consuming than flicking between the pages of a book. Not only can referencing information be obtained easily, but also without the loss of our original place in the hypertext (by 'backtracking'). Both of these advantages are likely to increase the occasions that such information is sought and read. Finally, the ethnography in hypertext form may facilitate the reader's critical appreciation of the author: upon reading a certain statement or proposition, the reader may explore how the author arrived at their theoretical position by following trails in the hypertext.

This final point brings us to one of the most important potentials of hypertext as a product of research: it alters the relation between reader and writer. Hypertext engenders the empowerment of readers since their interpretation of the text is not bounded by the way the ethnographer chose to structure it. For, as explained by Landow (1992, p. 11), 'hypertext does not permit a tyrannical, univocal voice. Rather the voice is always that distilled from the combined experience of the momentary focus, the lexia one presently reads, and the continually forming narrative of one's reading path'. Furthermore, since the published text also includes the analysis itself, readers can easily obtain the knowledge necessary to be critical of the grounds of a statement. Of course, this empowerment of the reader does not entail the disempowerment of the author, or even make the relationship equal. For ultimately, power still lies on the side of authors: they can take out from the hypertext parts of the analysis that they don't want readers to see. But it certainly seems that both reading and writing ethnography in hypertext form will encourage emerging theory to be substantially grounded in data, and that it will facilitate greater reflexivity. The issue of reflexivity, and how it relates to microcomputing strategies for qualitative data analysis, is one focus of the next and final chapter in this book.

6 Conclusion

This book has examined three analytic strategies inherent to three types of software. Drawing upon our experiences of analyzing the data with each program, we have attempted to compare and contrast their underlying assumptions, foregrounding their similarities and differences, and their implications for exploring qualitative data analytically. These more implicit aspects of microcomputing strategies, and their effect on qualitative analysis, had hitherto received little academic examination (there has certainly been little systematic comparison between them). Our work suggests that while some of the similarities and differences between programs are quite obvious (there are often clues in the name of the program and the range of functions it provides), others only emerge through empirical research. This chapter summarizes some of the conclusions of the research informing this book.

Focusing on what the three strategies have in common, we argue that all involve a transformation of data in some way. By utilizing a microcomputer program, a researcher accepts that analysis in itself constitutes a transformation of data: it is through organizing and recontextualizing data in different ways that knowledge of the data, or of social phenomena, is constructed. It may be argued perhaps that non-microcomputing strategies also involve these analytic activities. However, less obviously, various programs provide, or moreover assume, specific types of transformation. It may be argued here that although manual techniques of qualitative analysis involve some kind of transformation of data, they are probably more idiosyncratic. By contrast, with computer assisted data analysis, the range of options when choosing techniques is determined by the requirements and expectations of a particular set of algorithms built into a particular program. In short, each microcomputing strategy encourages the researcher to transform the data in a way that is different from all others. Through the comparison of strategies in this book, it is clear that the degree to which they differ varies. For example, coding has much in common with theory building strategies in the types of transformations it encourages, but hypertext embodies a different means of organizing data altogether. These transformations in turn encourage different ways of thinking about and characterizing data and theory.

The way that we think about data is not simply determined by their transformation produced by a computer program, of course: this is no simple relationship of cause and effect. For, in addition to computer programs, there are many contextual factors which help shape paths of analysis. For example, the knowledge and experiences that researchers bring to research are of vital methodological significance. In addition to material and situational constraints (such as technology, funding, geographical location), the backgrounds of researchers affect computer-assisted analysis at several levels. First, they have a profound impact on the program that researchers choose. Second, they affect the way that program is used. For although different programs produce different transformations of data, there is not only one way of doing analysis with either 'coding', 'lexical searching', 'theory building' or 'hypertext'. In other words, within one strategy there is room for many different 'substrategies'. This accommodates differences between researchers to some extent.

This point is most significant for hypertext, however. When using GUIDE, it is much less obvious how researchers should begin to transform and analyze the data than it was with ETHNOGRAPH. Indeed, it is precisely the openness and flexibility of hypertext which is likely to make it most attractive to inexperienced researchers. For researchers who are not accustomed to a particular analytic technique - such as copying, cutting and pasting segments of text (in which case ETHNOGRAPH would be the obvious choice of program) - GUIDE provides a microcomputing strategy that is at once disorientating but also intriguing and exciting. Allowing for spontancity and creativity, and thus encouraging diverse analytical approaches between its users, is one of the methodological merits of hypertext. However, it is also this aspect of hypertext that needs more research and methodological debate. The present study examines hypertext as a generic strategy, and the issues that were raised when it was applied to one particular case. But there is a need to study in more depth the various ways hypertext (and hypermedia) may be utilized, and this can only be achieved through the reflexive documentation of the experiences of various researchers using this strategy.

Despite being modelled on theories of human cognition, there is still much to be understood about hypertext. Its non-linear structure provides an approach to qualitative research that may revolutionize the means through which knowledge is constructed and represented. Conventional thinking is accomplished through the medium of reading and writing linear documents. Hypertext-type movement within and between such documents has always characterized research. However, without the help of electronic 'buttons', it is difficult or cumbersome to retrace spontaneous movements. Links are not therefore generally followed at another point in time in the pursuit of a whim or idea. This process has been made quicker and much more accurate with the advent of hypertext programs such as GUIDE, which automates these movements to such an extent that creating and following trails becomes the central analytic activity. Indeed, this is the chief way in which hypertext programs transform data.

However, hypertext has a different but related value for qualitative research. This concerns the nature in which the analytical work of one author is received by his/her peers. For not only are researchers' 'trails' of thought recorded for their own analytical needs, but also for the critical needs of others who are interested in analyzing the work. Thus pressure for the accountability of results is likely to be experienced to a far greater extent by hypertext accounts than printed accounts produced when using other types of software. Other strategies also encourage this 'accountability', but to a lesser extent. They too produce something - 'evidence' - that is tangible and concrete, and which is in a form that is easily amenable to the scrutiny of others. For example, with FYI and ETHNOGRAPH, this would be the printed searches on specific codes or words. But with linear accounts, the author has much more power in the way that evidence will be received by its audience. For example, authors have virtually all control over the order in which material is read. The question posed by Tesch (1990, p. 6) rarely arises: how would we know when we had 'finished the book'? Hypertext fits more closely to the Derridean conception of writing precisely for this reason: neither are linear processes with a clearly demarcated beginning and end (cf. Bolter, 1991; Landow, 1992).

Through their generation of evidence at various stages of analysis, or points in the transformation of data, it follows that all programs help to make explicit the ways in which researchers characterize data and develop hypotheses. But the way that they do this is qualitatively and quantitatively different. Printed searches on codes or lexical items make explicit and tangible the 'bones' of analysis, but hypertext goes beyond this: it also makes explicit the 'flesh', so to speak, or how researchers add meaning and make sense of the 'bones'. This is because, as already noted, hypertext makes explicit the thought process itself. Hypertext trails, like data, become objects (or 'bones', to return to the previous metaphor) in their own right, which in turn receive reflection and 'fleshing out' in due course.

It is important to consider how these conclusions, regarding the way these programs encourage researchers to think about data, relate to epistemological discourses. The most apparent connection here is how the programs differ in their relation to traditional objectivist and rationalist views of inquiry, on the one hand, and brands of social constructivism, on the other. The difference, in short, is whether one believes that there is an independently existing universe which knowledge represents, or whether the world and knowledge about it cannot be disentangled from social participants and social processes (Steir, 1991, p. 1). This is not a particularly new idea: it was argued by Nietzsche in the 1880s that theory and knowledge are forms of autobiography (Soderqvist, 1991, p. 148). But only relatively recently have its implications for social research been taken seriously.

The main methodological implication of social constructivism is that the presence of researchers needs to be acknowledged in social research, as this forms part of the social context in which meaning arises. This acknowledgement is embodied in the principle of 'reflexivity' or self-reference. Since its conception, this principle has become relatively well represented in social research regarding methods of data collection (such as interviewer effects). Its relevance to data analysis is not well documented, however. In this context, it is important to assess how the three analytic strategies accommodate reflexivity, and the extent to which researchers are aware of themselves, their decisions, their expectations, and how these shape research findings. Our research suggests that, because the ideas and trails of a researcher themselves become 'objects' in the same way as data, hypertext encourages thinking that is much more reflexive than that encouraged by other strategies. Researchers are encouraged to analyze and question their own ideas, and the emerging construction of knowledge, in the same way that they do their data. The issue of reflexivity is bound up with the broader question of how different transformations of data make researchers think differently about the text. The discussion will now turn to this important topic.

From our experience, it appears that ETHNOGRAPH may be used in two ways. First, it may be used for the purposes of gaining a holistic view of social phenomena by focusing on or 'slicing' the data in different ways, according to topics and themes. Alternatively, it may be used for the purposes of theorizing about aspects of the field or, in other words, how factors and variables relate to produce observed phenomena. Each approach to coding makes sense only in terms of different research aims and methodological considerations. Both were applied in this research because we wanted to keep as many avenues open as possible. We found that the way in which ETHNOGRAPH accommodates these strategies is contradictory.

In brief, ETHNOGRAPH is good for organizing data in terms of topics. This method of recontextualization, along with its mode of display which shows the other topics to which each segment is related, may encourage new insights about the data. Thus it is a useful tool for descriptive social research. But does this in itself constitute data analysis? The structure of ETHNOGRAPH implies that it does not: analysis also involves theory building. More specifically, the program assumes that theory building consists of constructing hypotheses about the relations between codes using Boolean operators. These are then to be tested against data by conducting multiple searches on codes. This facility loses its theoretical value when codes are general, abstract categories representing topics and themes. Thus, in ETHNOGRAPH'S theory building context, analysis is more effective if codes represent the causes, conditions, and consequences of social phenomena - variables - rather than topics. Multiple searching is only useful if we are interested in the relations between factors or variables in the field under study. Yet theory building by these means is very limited with ETHNOGRAPH because of its maximum limits regarding codes per segment, and only two types of Boolean operators. Moreover, this particular version of theory building is only comfortable with more traditional epistemological approaches, which value the construction and testing of hypotheses in the search for objective knowledge. Thus it seems that ETHNOGRAPH implicitly encourages an epistemological position which views the empirical or 'real' world of study, and data about it, as independent from the researcher.

Irrespective of either approach to analysis - descriptive or theoretical - our experience with ETHNOGRAPH questions the usefulness of its search facility. Its analytical worth certainly did not seem to justify the time-consuming work and problematic decision-making permeating data preparation (coding). However, the coding approach does yield some merits. In contrast to the assumed benefits of ETHNOGRAPH(enabling the searching of codes and the retrieval of relevant text), the value of the coding strategy seems to lie in the experience of constructing and applying an organizing system in the coding process. Searches appear to be more of a formality - for the tidying up and gathering of evidence for conclusion drawing - than processes giving rise to and exploring the main body of analytic insights. The process simply produces something concrete, and proves that the analysis is grounded in the data.

Second, Seidel's fear that researchers will become increasingly preoccupied with quantitative aspects of data - in particular volume and diversity - certainly seems to have taken hold. Our experience with ETHNOGRAPH suggests that both the amount and quality of attention given to topics or phenomena is often determined by the number of times their codes occur. Similarly, attention to the connection between topics or phenomena is often decided by the number of times that a given code occurs in a certain context (the frequency of other codes consistently being present or absent). These are the kinds of decisions encouraged (often implicitly) by ETHNOGRAPH. It takes a considerable effort for researchers to be reflective about such decisions, and to escape the 'sins' of reification. The dominance of a code throughout data does not necessarily imply the persistence of a variable over and above all others. For example, as we have argued, the quantitative predominance of a particular factor or phenomenon can be due to researchers having this factor or phenomenon in mind (when interacting with elements of the field while collecting data, or with the data during the coding process), and thereby perceiving the field or data in its terms.

Such questions tend to be ignored largely because the codes created by researchers all too easily become objects in their own right. Codes appear to be 'above' data somehow, to constitute something different: 'facts'. Unlike hypertext, which encourages the scrutiny of analytical or theoretical objects in the same way as data (no distinction is drawn between them by GUIDE),. ETHNOGRAPH encourages researchers to perceive codes differently from data. Indeed, ETHNOGRAPH only recognizes codes: it cannot read or manipulate the data directly as can FYI, NUDIST or GUIDE.

Furthermore, even if the researcher is reflexive in this sense (s/he acknowledges that coded data are likely represent knowledge brought to the field, or ideas that developed while collecting data or coding them), ETHNOGRAPH does not support the researcher in going beyond this acknowledgement and dealing with its constraints. Indeed, it is likely that, if this is the case, the researcher will want to reanalyze the data from a fresh 'perspective', in which newly emerging themes may dominate the collection, coding, and search processes. ETHNOGRAPH offers little support here because it relies on a linear research process: this strategy has no value until a substantial amount of data has been coded with a substantial number of codes. A fresh perspective cannot be achieved without effectively recoding the entire data set in terms of this perspective. Thus, whereas ETHNOGRAPH may be a useful tool in qualitative research for some researchers, for others it will prove to be frustrating, and consequently little value may be attached to the program as a 'tool' for analysis. This seems to be especially the case for those sympathetic to a brand of social constructivism, where reflexivity is considered an important methodological issue.

Similar frustrations were encountered in our research. While using ETHNOGRAPH, we concluded that the material product of the coding process - the coded data - was not in fact very meaningful. Coded data were not in line with the 'ideal' product, so to speak, because they did not represent our knowledge of the data adequately enough. Rather, they reflected the chronological development of ideas. Even if we were to recode the data, it would again be a linear, cumulative process, and our ideas about categories will have changed by the end of it. In other words, researchers felt alienated from the coded data because they did not reflect consistently the knowledge that had accumulated by the end of the coding process; familiarity with data progressed more quickly than the analysis process could accommodate. Thus it was often found that the interpretations embedded in these representations were inappropriate or seemed rather 'thin' or simplistic. Coded data did not, therefore, provide a useful basis for further analysis, including that embedded in the activities of searching and retrieving of data in a theory building context.

Indeed, it may be argued that the coding strategy is at odds with reflexivity, to some extent, because whereas the former requires linear processes, the latter requires circular ones. Hypertext, seems to be better suited to reflexive research for this very reason. Consider the following description of 'self-reflective' activity by Gergen and Gergen (1991, p. 91) regarding their research on the meaning of photographs without narrative:

> Like a geometric pattern, the photo series had become the point of origin, each reflexive phase was a loop, circling out and then returning to the core. Each circle took on a new direction - and with each line the rosette became increasingly complex.

The assumptions embedded in ETHNOGRAPH are not suited to this task. GUIDE was not designed to accommodate the needs of reflexivity either. But because hypertext programs mimic the structure of human cognition a reflexive circle or analytic trail is represented in the hypertext in the same way as a train of thought or memory trail in the human mind. Thus, each of Gergen and Gergen's (1991, p. 88) 'loops' constitutes a hypertext trail radiating to and from the data. Each trail is like a different narrative, connecting modes of information which otherwise, like Gergen and Gergen's photographs, would be meaningless. Thus, programs such as GUIDE facilitates the 'reflexive elaboration of the event' by representing a dialogue between different 'voices', perspectives, or narratives in the form of hypertext trails.

Indeed, with hypertext, there may be a dialogue not only between different voices or perspectives constructed by one author, but between those of a number of authors. This offers new possibilities in the application of microcomputers to collaborative research. Furthermore, readers can also become authors in the 'reflexive circle'. 'In principle, the spiral knows no boundaries. With socially reflective research one need never say"goodbye"' (Gergen and Gergen, 1991, p. 93). These possibilities of hypertext pose new and interesting relations and boundaries between the conventional roles of those who engage in and consume social research, and thus deserve to be the focus of future empirical research.

Hypertext's accommodation of reflexive activity encourages researchers to see not only data as variable, in that their meaning depends upon a certain frame of reference, but also the evaluations of data by a given researcher, for the same reasons. Hypertext may reinforce in social research the tenet of social constructivism, described by Gergen and Gergen (1991, p. 89), that narrative forms guide an understanding and appreciation of, not only self, but also what people find tedious or interesting. From this perspective, such issues must be considered in social research. Just as researchers may be interested in why participants in the field find certain activities exciting, they must apply the same questions to themselves. Field events only make sense in the context of particular narratives. So do the elements of research findings and practice.

If one subscribes to the tenets of social constructivism - that it is only by recourse to narrative forms that events are given meaning, or that meaning is not inherent to an event - issues become more complicated with hypermedia systems. For not only is there 'narrativity' which is generic to text, but also 'camerativity' if photographs are scanned into the database, or 'filmativity' if video material is used. The point here is that each technology used in data analysis or for the representation of knowledge has its own particular structure. In the same way that researchers have to be reflexive about the perspectives they throw on data, they also have to be reflexive about the perspectives or representations inherent to each technology utilized in their research. The new complications introduced into research by hypermedia are not necessarily undesirable however. For, as suggested by Gergen and Gergen (1991, p. 92), perhaps no single technology, or even a combination of technologies, can produce a totally accurate representation of reality. Indeed, hypermedia introduces the electronic triangulation of representations into qualitative analysis. However, although the technology to do this is there, 'an appropriate methodology of representation has not yet emerged' (Seaman and Williams, 1992, p. 301).

163

Just as the tape recorder or video camera provide different ways of knowing 'reality', in how they relate researchers to their field of study, the programs studied in this book provide different ways of knowing 'data', in the way they structure the relationship between researchers and data. With ETHNOGRAPH, this relationship is conditioned by codes, with FYI it is by the lexical content of data, and with hypertext it is in terms of electronic trails. However, hypertext trails may weave together not only various segments of fieldnotes or their constituent words, but also analytic notes and memoranda, and even sources of information that are external to the research at hand, such as excerpts from other research. Thus hypertext facilitates a way of 'knowing' data that is much more encompassing and multifaceted than the other two strategies. However, there is also a fundamental similarity shared by the strategies. In all of them, spatial relations between the various objects of analysis (whether codes, words, or buttons) are of vital importance because they point to conceptual relations.

Programs also affect the relation between analysis and the 'writing up' of research. It is expected that the linearity imposed on analysis by ETHNOGRAPH in principle makes this transition much more straightforward than with the other two programs. Users of hypertext in particular, because it encourages a non-linear analytic process, are likely to find the transition problematic. (Unless, of course, the material product of analysis - the ethnographic monograph for example - is to be published in hypertext form.) Issues raised in the transition from analysis using microcomputing strategies to authoring need to be the object of future empirical research.

Much of the research reported in this book has focused on the nature of technical issues encountered when using programs. Although this was not a primary aim of the study, it is important that technical problems are documented because they constitute an important part of the methodological context. Just as problems relating to negotiating access, for example, should be discussed in method chapters, there is also a need for researchers to make explicit their decisions when confronted with technical problems or, in other words, how analyses are tailored to fit programs. This is because the way researchers encounter and resolve technical problems is an important part of the research process and has methodological consequences. We found that working with ETHNOGRAPH necessitated these kinds of decisions to a far greater extent than the others. Indeed, concern with technical issues consumed a considerable amount of time devoted to analysis.

The other issue needing reiteration is that it is not always apparent how programs are most effectively used. This is, of course, related to the extent to which they impose structure on analysis. ETHNOGRAPH does this fairly rigidly: we must divide the data into chunks and code it by hand before we can enter codes into the program, and we must key codes into the program before we can search for coded segments. As with KWALITAN and NUDIST, we know that analysis consists of devising symbols (codes or keywords) to represent concepts, attaching them to text, and manipulating them in various ways to produce their interrelationships. Researchers accustomed to these approaches to analysis will feel disorientated in an initial encounter with GUIDE, however. This is because these aspects of structure which give meaning to what we do (code), how we do it (by attaching categories to segments of text), and why (to recontextualize text in analytically meaningful ways by searching for conjunctions of codes) are missing. GUIDE does not demand that data be structured in any particular way, and it is not immediately obvious how one should use its tools to structure analysis. Indeed this fact, combined with the potential hazards of losing track of objects and links in 'hyperspace', demands a very well organized thinker.

This is not to belittle the imaginative and organizational skills required in the other strategies, or to imply that analysis with those programs are mechanical. Indeed, constructing dictionaries and thesauri for FYI, and overcoming the technical limitations of ETHNOGRAPH in coding and searching, are but a few of the tasks which require insight, imagination and skill using other strategies. On the contrary, a recognition of these different types of problems gives rise to a general methodological point. Although programs for qualitative analysis tend to be considered as tools for improving methods of organizing data, they do not in any respect diminish the organizational responsibility and skills of their users. Unorganized researchers will not prosper simply because they have utilized microcomputing strategies, rather than manual methods, of qualitative analysis. Similarly, a researcher who is particularly skilled and organized using one strategy is not necessarily so using another.

This brings the present discussion to a final methodological point - one that has implications for our research findings. Programs do not shape analyses in any conclusive or absolute way because researchers interact differently with them. Nevertheless, there is certainly a need for researchers to be reflective about their experiences of specific programs when analyzing various types of qualitative data. This is because the decision to use a program in the first place (let alone how it is implemented to analyze data), has significant consequences for research outcomes. The documentation and discussion of such experiences is also important at the more general level of methodological debate. But while the latter is necessary, it is unlikely that discussions will be 'conclusive' as such. We have argued that microcomputing strategies and - even less - particular programs within these genres, do not fully determine analysis. This undermines the generalizability of the conclusions embodied in this book to some extent, and it should not be read for these ends. But its original purpose still stands. The study represents one collaborative attempt to reflect on the way microcomputing strategies influence the way data and analysis were approached, and to make explicit the assumptions, decisions, and processes that were encouraged by these strategies, in one particular piece of research.

Bibliography

Agar, M. (1983), 'Microcomputers as Field Tools', *Computers in the Humanities*, 17, pp. 19-26.

Altheide, D.L. (1985), 'Keyboarding as a Social Form', *Computers and the Social Sciences*', No. 3.

Atkinson, P. (1990), *The Ethnographic Imagination: Textual Constructions of Reality*, Routledge, London.

Atkinson, P. (1991), ESRC research proposal, *Microcomputing and Qualitative Analysis*.

Atkinson, P. (1992), 'The ethnography of a medical setting: reading, writing, and rhetoric', *Qualitative Health Research*, Vol. 2, No. 4, pp. 451-474.

Becker, H.S. (1994), 'The Uses of Hypertext', *Writing Sociology*, Vol. 1, No. 3, p. 6.

Becker, H.S., Gordon, A.C. and LeBailly, R.K. (1984), 'Fieldwork with the Computer: Criteria for Assessing Systems', *Qualitative Sociology*, Vol. 7, No. 1-2, pp. 16-33.

Benest, I.D. (1990), 'A Hypertext System with Controlled Hype', in McAleese, R. and Green, C. (eds) *Hypertext: State of the Art*, Intellect, Oxford.

Blank, G. (1988), 'New Technology and the Nature of Sociological Work', *American Sociologist*, Vol. 19, No. 3, pp. 3-15.

Blank, G. (1989), 'Introduction', in Blank, G. et al. (eds), *New Technology in Sociology: Practical Applications in Research and Work*, Transaction, New Brunswick, NJ.

Bolter, J.D. (1991), *Writing Space: the computer, hypertext, and the history of writing*, Lawrence Erlbraum Associates, Hillsdale, NJ.

Burgess, R.G. (1984), *In the Field*, George Allen and Unwin, London.

Burkholder, L. (1992), 'Computers and Philosophy: the state of the art', *Computers and Texts*, Newsletter No. 3. pp. 5-7.

Christensen, B.M. (1992), 'Conceptual Understanding By Use of

Computers', presented to the International Human Science Research Association Conference.

Conklin, J. (1987), 'Hypertext: An Introduction and Survey',*Computer*, 20, Sept, pp. 17-44.

Conrad, P. and Reinharz, S. (1984), 'Computers and Qualitative Data', *Qualitative Sociology*, Vol. 7, No. 1-2, pp. 3-15

Cordingley, E.S. (1991), 'The Upside and Downside of Hypertext Tools: the KANT example', in Fielding, N.G. and Lee, R.M. (eds) *Using Computers in Qualitative Research*, Sage, London.

Davies, J. (1991), 'Automated Tools for Qualitative Analysis', in Fielding, N.G. and Lee, R.M. (eds)*Using Computers in Qualitative Research*, Sage, London.

Dey, I. (1993), *Qualitative Data Analysis: a user-fiendly guide for social scientists*, Routledge, London.

Drass, K.A. (1989), 'Text-Analysis software: A Comparison of Assumptions', in Blank, G. et Al (eds) *New Technology in Sociology: Practical Applications in Research and Work*, Transaction, New Brunswick, NJ.

Fielding N.G. (1993), 'Qualitative Data Analysis with a computer: recent developments', *Social Research Update*, Issue 1.

Fielding N.G. and Lee R.M. (eds) (1991), *Using Computers in Qualitative Research*, Sage, London.

Gergen, K.J. and Gergen, M.M. (1991), 'Toward Reflexive Methodologies', in Steier, F. (ed) *Research and Reflexivity*, Sage, London.

Glaser, B. and Strauss, A.L. (1967), *The Discovery of Grounded Theory: Strategies for Qualitative Research*, Aldine, Chicago.

Hammersley, M. and Atkinson, P. (1983), *Ethnography: principles in practice, Routledge*, Routledge, London.

Harper (1989), 'Visual Sociology: expanding sociological vision', in Blank, G. et Al (eds) *New Technology in Sociology: Practical Applications in Research and Work*, Transaction, New Brunswick, NJ.

Hesse-Biber, S., Dupius, P. and Kinder, S. (1989), 'HYPEResearch: A Computer Program for the Analysis of Qualitative Data Using the Macintosh', presented to the Annual meeting of the American Sociological Association, San Francisco.

Heise, D.R. (1991), 'Event Structure Analysis: A Qualitative Model of Quantitative Research', in Fielding, N.G. and Lee, R.M. (eds) *Using Computers in Qualitative Research*, Sage, London.

Jonassen, D.H. (1990), 'Semantic Network Elicitation: Tools for Structuring Hypertext', in McAleese, R. and Green, C. (eds) *Hypertext: State of the Art*, Intellect, Oxford.

168

Krippendorff, K. (1980), *Content Analysis: An Introduction to its Methodology*, Sage, London.

Landow, G.P. (1992), *Hypertext: the convergence of contemoprary critical theory and technology*, Johns Hopkins University Press, London.

Lofland (1971), *Analyzing Social Settings: a guide to qualitative observation and analysis*, Wadsworth, Belmont, CA.

Lyman, P. (1984), 'Reading, Writing and Wordprocessing: Toward a Phenomenology of the Computer Age', *Qualitative Sociology*, Vol. 7 No. 1-2, pp. 75-89.

Lyman, P. (1989), 'The Future of Sociological Literature in an Age of Computerized Texts', in Blank, G. et Al (eds) *New Technology in Sociology: Practical Applications in Research and Work*, Transaction, New Brunswick, NJ.

Mayes, T., Kibby, M.R., and Anderson, A. (1990), 'Signposts for Conceptual Orientation: Some Requirements for Learning from Hypertext', in McAleese, R. and Green, C. (eds) *Hypertext: State of the Art*, Intellect, Oxford.

Miles, M.B. and Huberman, A.M. (1984), *Qualitative Data Analysis: A Sourcebook of New Methods*, Sage, Beverly Hills, CA.

Peters, V. and Wester, F. (1990), *Kwalitan: a user's guide*, Department of Research Methodology, University of Nijmegen, the Netherlands.

Pfaffenberger, B. (1988), *Microcomputer Applications in Qualitative Research*, Sage, Beverly Hills, CA

Rada, R. (1991), *Hypertext: from text to expertext*, McGraw-Hill, Maidenhead.

Ragin, C.C. and Becker, H.S. (1989), 'How the Microcomputer is Changing our Analytic Habits', in Blank, G. et Al (eds) *New Technology in Sociology: Practical Applications in Research and Work*, Transaction, New Brunswick, NJ.

Read, D.W. (1990), 'Anthropology and Computers: Promise and Potential', *Social Science Computer Review*, Vol. 8, No. 4, pp. 503-514.

Richards et al (1990a), *NUDIST 2.3 User Manual*, Replee P/L in association with La Trobe University, Bundoora, Vic.

Richards L. and Richards, T. (1987), 'Qualitative Data Analysis: can computers do it', *Australian and New Zealand Journal of Sociology*, Vol. 23, No. 1, pp. 23-35.

Richards et al (1990b), *NUDIST 2.3 Reference Manual*, Replee Pty Ltd in association with La Trobe University, Bundoora, Vic.

Richards, L. and Richards, T. (1991a), 'The Transformation of Qualitative Method: Computational Paradigms and Research Processes', in Fielding,N.G. and Lee, R.M. (eds) *Using Computers in Qualitative*

Research, Sage, London.

Richards, T. and Richards L. (1991b), 'Computing in Qualitative Analysis: A Healthy Development?', *Qualitative Health Research*, Vol. 1, No. 2, pp. 234-262.

Roth, J. (1957), 'Ritual and Magic in the Control of Contagion', *American Sociological Review*, Vol. 22, pp. 310-14.

Roth, J. (1963), *Timetables*, Bobbs-Merrill Company, New York.

Seaman G. and Williams, H. (1992), 'Hypermedia in ethnography', in Crawford, P. and Turton, D. (eds), *Film as Ethnography*, Manchester University Press, Manchester.

Seidel, J. (1988), *The Ethnograph: a user's guide*, Qualis Research Associates, Littleton, CO.

Seidel, J.V. (1991), 'Method and Madness in the Application of Computer Technology to Qualitative Data Analysis', in Fielding, N.G. and Lee, R.M. (eds) *Using Computers in Qualitative Research*, Sage, London.

Shipman, M.D. (1981), *The Limitations of Social Research*, Longman, New York.

Silverman, D. (1993), *Interpreting Qualitative Data: methods of analysing talk, text and interaction*, Sage, London.

Soderqvist (1991), 'Biography or Ethnobiography or Both? Embodied Reflexivity and the Deconstruction of Knowledge-Power', in Steier, F. (ed) *Research and Reflexivity*, Sage, London. Steier (1991), 'Introduction: Research as Self-Reflexivity, Self- Reflexivity as Social Process', in Steier, F. (ed) *Research and Reflexivity*, Sage, London.

Stark, H.A. (1990), 'What do Readers do to Pop-Ups and Pop-Ups do to Readers?', in McAleese, R. and Green, C. (eds) *Hypertext: State of the Art*, Intellect, Oxford.

√ Strauss, A.L. (1987), *Qualitative Analysis for Social Scientists*, Cambridge University Press, Cambridge.

Tesch, R. (1989), 'Computer Software and Qualitative Analysis: A Reassessment' in Blank, G. et Al (eds) *New Technology in Sociology: Practical Applications in Research and Work*, Transaction Books, New Brunswick, NJ.

Tesch, R. (1990), Qualitative Research: *Analysis Types and Software Tools*, Falmer Press, London.

Tesch, R. (1991), 'Software for Qualitative Researchers: Anlaysis Needs and Program Capabilities' in Fielding, N.G. and Lee, R.M. (eds) *Using Computers in Qualitative Research*, Sage, London.

Thomas, J. (19) 'Catching up to the cyber age', *Writing Sociology*, Vol. 1, No. 2, pp. 1-2.

Wagner, R.A. (1989), 'The Rise of Computing in Anthropology: Hammers and Nails', *Social Science and Computer Review*, Vol. 7, No. 4, pp. 418-430.

Walker, B.L. (1993), 'Computer Analysis of Qualitative Data: A Comparrison of Three Packages', *Qualitative Health Research*, Vol 3, No. 1, pp. 91-111.

Walker, R. and Bryman A. (1991), 'Styles of Qualitative Analysis: an examination and evaluation', *Centre for Research in Social Policy*, Loughborough University, Loughborough.

Weaver, A. (1994), 'Deconstructing Dirt and Disease: the case of TB', in M. Bloor and P. Tarraborelli (eds) *Qualitative Studies in Health and Medicine*, Avebury, Aldershot.

Weitzman, E. and Miles, M.B. (1994), *Computer Programs for Qualitative Data Analysis*, Sage, Thousand Oaks, CA.

White, D.R. and Truex, G.F. (1988), 'Anthropology and Computing: The Challenges of the 1990s', *Social Science Computer Review*, Vol. 6, No. 4, pp. 481-497.

Wood, M. (1984), 'Using Key-Word-In-Context Concordance Programs for Qualitative and Quantitative Social Research', *Journal of Applied Behavioural Science*, Vol. 20, No. 3, pp. 289-297.